JAMIE FOREMAN

ON THE RUN

JAME FOREMAN

ON THE RUN

NOW HE'S A MOVIE STAR ...
BUT ONCE, HE AND HIS NOTORIOUS
FATHER LIVED BY THE GUN.
THIS IS HIS TRUE STORY.

JB

JOHN BLAKE

Published by John Blake Publishing Ltd,
3 Bramber Court, 2 Bramber Road,
London W14 9PB, England

www.johnblakepublishing.co.uk

First published in hardback in 2009

ISBN: 978 1 84454 822 4

British Library Cataloguing-in-Publication Data:

A catalogue record for this book is available from the British Library.

Design by www.envydesign.co.uk

Printed in the UK by CPI William Clowes, Beccles NR34 7TL

1 3 5 7 9 10 8 6 4 2

Papers used by John Blake Publishing are natural, recyclable products
made from wood grown in sustainable forests. The manufacturing processes
conform to the environmental regulations of the country of origin.

Every attempt has been made to contact the relevant copyright-holders, but
some were unobtainable. We would be grateful if the appropriate people
could contact us.

To my mother and father, Julie and my boys

ACKNOWLEDGEMENTS

To everyone at John Blake Publishing for this
wonderfully cathartic experience, especially John and
the lovely Michelle. With special thanks to Mark
Hanks and Jo: cheers, Mark, for everything – couldn't
have done it without you.

CONTENTS

CONTENTS

THE WAY IT WAS

I was brought up to be what we call a 'straight goer'. I was taught to live my life honestly and not to do anything wrong. I was raised to be a good boy. To behave myself at all times and never to take anything that didn't belong to me.

Yet taking things that didn't belong to him was exactly what my father went out and did every day. You could call it a moral paradox, but to me it was just the world I was born into. Dad did what he did to put food on our table and clothes on our backs. He did it because he wanted a slice of the good life and he had no other means of getting it. It was what he did; he loved the buzz and that's the way it was. There are no two ways about it. I come from a criminal background and I can't say I'm ashamed of it.

I was born the second son of one of London's most successful gangsters, Freddie Foreman. He had been at it for years before I came along and, wherever he went, his reputation preceded him. For years my dad had been involved in some of Britain's most audacious armed robberies, and dealing with the most dangerous criminals working in Britain. It was his world, and there was no way my arrival on the scene would change that.

Not that I had much of a clue about what he did. I was just a kid and my dad was, well, just my dad. He might have been out grafting and building his reputation, but it didn't mean Dad wasn't there to tuck in his kids at night with a story and a kiss. One of my earliest memories is the rustle of his mohair and silk suit, the faint smell of brandy on his breath, his strong, masculine aftershave and the feeling that I didn't have a worry in the world. Dad was always there for us. There would come a time when I'd need to be there for him, but that was later. Much later.

'Us' was my mum, Maureen, my older brother Gregory and my younger sister Danielle, and, although we moved about a bit when I was young, my childhood really got going in Kennington, South London. We lived in Braun House on the Brandon council estate in a lovely, newly built high-rise flat and, at six years old, I wouldn't have wanted to be anywhere else in the world.

It sounds like a cliché, but I was born into a time when the indomitable spirit of the British was at its strongest. The adults surrounding me had survived the war and the ensuing austerity. They had seen their neighbourhoods destroyed – there were bombsites on every corner (which made great playgrounds for us kids) – they had run out of food and lost loved ones in the blitzed London streets as well as on foreign fields. Yet they were bonded by values that nowadays are being sadly eroded. There was a marvellous sense of togetherness among the working classes – you didn't steal from your own, you didn't hurt your own and, yes, you *did* leave your front door unlocked. It really did happen, I promise. I remember two old sisters who allowed me and my mates to walk into their flat through the back door and make ourselves a sugar sandwich whenever we pleased. The only rule was that you never went past the kitchen. We never broke that rule, nor did it ever enter our minds to.

In those days, council flats were something to be proud of. All the women used to clean their front steps and the landings, and the only smell on any block was that of Jeyes Fluid. That lovely, clean smell of antiseptic just about summed up how houseproud and respectable most people were back then.

Not that I spent much time around the house. When I wasn't at Henry Fawcett Primary School, I was mostly off playing with my mates. There was no better place to play than the streets. We'd be out from dawn to dusk, forever inventing new games, fighting new battles. I saw my fair share of fights, but they were mainly between older kids. I could hold my own and was always a good puncher. But I never had a fight with anyone smaller than me. Mind you, there weren't many people smaller than me.

If it wasn't Mum calling me in at night, it would be my lovely auntie Nell, a pivotal member of the family. My Nell was a 'Spitfire' – small, feisty and beautiful. She looked after me when Mum and Dad needed to keep me 'at a safe distance'. There's no denying that Dad's business meant it was sometimes best if I was temporarily out of harm's way. But it didn't bother me one bit – spending time with my Nell and my two beautiful cousins, Barbie and Geraldine, was always a joy. Barbie was like a big sister to me, and I loved her dearly. Nell would take me shopping down Lambeth Walk and then to the pie and mash shop – my favourite. Still is today. She was always fussing over me with the best food she could afford. I remember sitting in her tiny council flat in Lambeth North with her and my other aunts watching the Saturday-afternoon films on BBC2 while they drank tea and smoked cigarettes. You could have cut the smoke with a knife. I just loved sitting there with my gorgeous, indomitable aunts watching *A Tree Grows In Brooklyn* or some other weepy, and seeing them by turns crying, laughing and gossiping about anything and everyone the films reminded them of. They often talked of the war and, although there were plenty of painful memories, it inspired such awe in me when I saw them laughing the past away together. Those precious afternoons played a huge part in teaching me to laugh in the face of adversity.

Becoming aware of what Dad did, and of his power in the criminal underworld, was a gradual process. I would have had to be blind, deaf and dumb to think that he was a regular man working regular hours in a regular job. However, as a kid, I wasn't told any more about him than I needed to know. And the truth was, I didn't need to know much. Not that I wasn't interested. The older I got, the more fascinated by the mystery of it all I became. As a result I was a sponge for everything that happened around me. It was like being a detective in one of the movies I loved – Humphrey Bogart in *The Big Sleep*, say – only the case I was working was my life, and it was anything but dull.

I remember walking with my auntie Nell down Lambeth Walk one day, and a man stopped me in the street. I must have been five or six years old, and I could immediately sense the alert in Nell. She obviously recognised the bloke as one of Dad's enemies, and immediately created a bit of a brouhaha before stealing me swiftly away. It was incidents like this, combined with my dad's insistence that I always told him where I was going, that made me realise I had to be on my toes when I was out and about. That is still true today. No one told me I was unsafe – I'm sure Dad always had me covered without telling me – but to certain people the Foremans were a prime target and I was taught not to take anything, or anyone, for granted. It was a valuable lesson that has stayed with me all my life. I developed a sixth sense for smelling a dangerous situation, and it would help me through many a tight spot in the future.

There was plenty more for me to soak up when Dad moved us from our council flat into one of his new businesses, the Prince of Wales public house in Lant Street in the Borough. It was so exciting for a seven-year-old. To say my dad owned a pub was a big step up in my social circle – being the son of the local publican gave me a great degree of kudos with my mates that I have to admit I liked. Of course, there was another side to the enterprise that I was only dimly aware of back then. As well as being a good money earner, the pub was a good front.

It was at the pub that I began to get more of an inkling about who, and what, my father was. Criminal or not, Dad was a man who didn't take kindly to bad manners. And it soon became clear that, as a landlord, he wouldn't have these principles trifled with. My mum told me that, soon after we moved in, he had a run-in with the local bully, who obviously didn't know who my dad was. One day Dad was laughing and joking with some customers at one end of the bar while the bully was playing darts down the other end.

'Quiet down there,' said the bully, pointing a finger at my father. 'Man at the oche.'

Dad glanced up, the smile vanishing from his face. Mum sighed. Something was about to happen, and it wasn't going to be the start of a beautiful friendship. All the signs were there – Dad was icy cool, calm and collected, with that flicker of anger in his eye. Not great news.

Casually, Dad walked across the pub, past the bully and up to the dartboard, which he ripped from the wall. He opened the door to the pub, walked outside and threw it on to the street. He'd been meaning to get rid of that dartboard, so I suppose this was as good a time as any. It might have ended there, but while my dad was outside the stupid sod who'd started it all decided to shut the pub door and lean on it. He was trying to shut my dad out of his own pub. Mum sighed again. Now there would definitely be trouble.

Dad charged the door, which burst open and sent the bloke flying. Quick as a flash, Dad picked him up, knocked him spark out with one punch and slung him out the door.

'No more darts in here,' he said, dusting his hands off before resuming his chat with the customers. Before long, laughter filled the room again.

There was a body and a dartboard in the street. Word soon got around with the locals that Dad wasn't to be messed with.

The pub quickly became a South London hotspot. Everyone used to go to the Prince of Wales, but they all called it Foreman's. It was a lovely little place – red flock wallpaper from Sanderson, wood half-panelling on each wall and, on one of them, a beautiful 16th-century map of London. Around the walls hung silhouettes of Dickens characters – Uriah Heep, Mr Bumble, Bill Sykes and Oliver Twist surveyed us all. Dickens was significant because the great man himself had once resided in Lant Street when his father was in Marshalsea Debtors' Prison just around the corner. The house Dickens lodged in had been demolished, but Dad had acquired its lock and key and proudly displayed it in a glass case. I even attended the local primary school called – you guessed it – Charles Dickens Primary. Little did I know that one day I'd play one of literature's greatest villains, Bill Sykes, in Roman Polanski's film of *Oliver Twist*.

Foreman's was the first pub in South London to have a wall-mounted jukebox. It played all of the latest releases before they hit the charts, thanks to the A.1 Stores in Walworth Road. They made sure you heard it first in the Prince of Wales. The atmosphere was always electric. It was the kicking-off place for young people's nights out before heading off to clubs in Herne Hill, Hammersmith, Streatham or the West End. Young 'faces' from the manor – the Elephant and Castle, Walworth Road and Bermondsey – would come in with their beautiful girlfriends and the place had a sexual charge that was any young boy's dream. I'll never forget how it felt walking through the bar and being grabbed by all these pretty young women who wanted to say hello to little Jamie. By the time I'd crossed the bar I'd have lipstick marks all over me, and I loved it.

Dad's business extended further than just selling beer, but that didn't mean it was a pub full of criminals. His 'firm' used to congregate there, of course, but they happily rubbed shoulders with the rest of the young crowd. No one needed to know that they were calling in favours and doing a bit of business at the same time. My godfather Buster Edwards and the other Great Train Robbers would often drop by, as would the Krays, who were good friends, especially Charlie and his beautiful wife Dolly. But the customers were none the wiser and the atmosphere was always lively and happy.

My dad and his firm were precisely why Foreman's had a reputation for being such a safe pub. You could take your girlfriend there and be secure in the knowledge that nobody was going to take liberties with you. No one ever caused any trouble. They didn't dare. If anyone was about to perform, the chances were they'd be dealt with before it even kicked off and slung out without ceremony – the 'chaps' could smell trouble at a thousand yards. Dad's pitch was always in the corner of the pub, so he could see everything that was going on. As a result, the atmosphere wasn't tense: it was fantastic.

The sixties were in full swing, and our pub seemed to

represent that – it was a melting pot of classes and personalities. Pop stars such as Cat Stevens and Manfred Mann were regulars, as was the great footballer Bobby Moore and his wife, along with other West Ham, Spurs, Millwall and Chelsea stars. Actors and actresses – especially Barbara Windsor and the *Carry On* team – mixed freely with High Court judges and politicians. A highlight was when the legendary Hollywood star George Raft was in town and spent the day drinking with my mum and dad. Unfortunately, the Home Office deemed Mr Raft unsuitable to stay in the country and he was deported back to the States. I wish I could have met him. Still, I have some great photographs of them together.

All manner of men and women came to the pub and had a great time. Young as I was, I sensed that Dad had extensive connections and interests that went far beyond anything I could fully understand. I was part of it, in as much as I was a Foreman, and I used to feel as if I was linked to something slightly nefarious and secretive. It was exciting and exhilarating, and it made me feel protected and safe.

I observed the kind of network that was growing around my father and I began to understand the reputation he had. Moreover, I learned that a man in that world has nothing but his reputation and his name. The values my dad and his firm adhered to were strong: you never fuck anyone over for money; you never hurt one of your own; you never take liberties with anybody; you never bully and most importantly you never, *ever*, grass. In those days there was more honour among thieves. And, while I was no thief, I grew up around men whose values I had nothing but respect for.

Everyone accepts and adapts to their surroundings, and that's what I did as a boy. I can't condemn anyone I've grown up with and loved all my life. My family, my uncles (the men close to me who I call uncles), they were all products of their environment and products of their day. Their lives took them down a certain path, and if they were horrible people I would have recognised it by now. They were strong and dangerous people, yes, but they were also kind, generous and caring men. There were equally strong and dangerous men on the other side of the fence – the firms that were the enemy. That was life, and to me what I experienced as a boy was merely part of London's rich tapestry.

Crime may have been exciting. It may have meant money and power. It may have been the thing that made my dad feel alive. But Freddie Foreman did not want his son to follow in his footsteps. He wanted better things for me.

Dad and I have always had a special relationship. Behind the scenes he was tender, caring and very keen to educate me and make me think. He never once raised a hand to me – he ruled with the mind, not the rod. When telling me off, he would make me see the error of my ways. He always spoke to me as an adult, and introduced me to adult things – from Beethoven to Buddy Greco, Frank Capra to William Shakespeare. Sure, he'd get down on the floor and play soldiers with me, but he would lay out the battle lines with care, and regale me with stories about tactics and great battles. He stimulated my mind and instilled a love of the theatrical in me.

Dad was simply the best dad he could be. As a child I felt such warmth and love that, when my parents told me I had a place at boarding school, I trusted that it was the right move. And, as always, my trust in them wasn't misplaced.

BETWEEN TWO WORLDS

Three pairs of brown socks, three pairs of black socks, three pairs of long socks and three pairs of short socks; three pairs for cricket, three for football and rugby. And then there were the pants, pyjamas, shirts and short trousers.

My tearful mum and I packed all the kit into my new trunk. Christ, I thought, I really am going on the adventure of a lifetime. I was seven years old. In my head it was as if I was getting ready to embark on a journey to distant lands – India, Africa perhaps. In reality I would soon be greeted by a stern matron and even sterner headmaster at Christ's College Preparatory School in Blackheath, South-east London. The Regency-

style, flat-fronted building I turned up to might as well
have been on the other side of the planet, yet ironically
it was less than half-an-hour's drive from the pub.

Where I came from, it wasn't exactly the norm to go to
a private school, but the lifestyle Mum and Dad had
achieved wasn't exactly the norm either. My older
brother Gregory had gone there a couple of years before
me, which made it easier for me to get in, but I'm sure a
little bit of skulduggery helped secure my place. I later
found out Dad knew one of the governors, and it was a
case of the old 'not what you know, but who you know'
working its magic. Still, I remember the interviews, and
especially Mum and Dad speaking a bit posh and trying
to make a good impression, and the memory of that
always makes me smile.

Our parents wanted the best for us kids, and sending
us to good schools was part of getting it. It was a case of
giving us a good start so we didn't end up going down
other roads. I'd say I was sent to boarding school for my
betterment, to make a man of me. I knew how loved I
was and I didn't resent Mum and Dad one bit for taking
me out of my familiar environment and giving me a new
direction. I understood, and I also knew that Dad saw
boarding school as a way of keeping me safe from harm.
He operated in a dangerous world and he didn't want
me to get caught up in it.

Christ's College wasn't Eton, but it was certainly run
along similar lines. Structure, discipline, fraternity, self-

discipline and an all-round education were the order of the day. The school, which had a long tradition dating back to the 1880s, catered for a broad range of types – from 'old money' to kids like me representing the emerging class of people who could suddenly afford fee-paying schools, to sons of international diplomats and the Persian aristocracy. Being surrounded by such a wide spectrum of people from different cultures taught me how to get on with just about anyone, no matter what their background. It didn't matter who you were or where you came from: once you donned the red blazer you were all equal.

I was used to being away from my parents round Auntie Nell's, but starting at the school was still a bit of a shock, to put it mildly. Until then I'd always done pretty much what I wanted, and suddenly I was being shown around an alien environment by an older boy with a posh accent and having rules drummed into me. And the rules were mostly things you couldn't do, of course. I could hardly believe it when I was told bedtime was 6.30pm, when I'd been used to scampering home whenever it got dark. The endless regulations weren't exactly music to my ears, yet over time I came to find them strangely reassuring. There's something about boundaries that kids need and respect. It gives their lives structure. Christ's College Prep School is where I learned that and it certainly stood me in good stead.

My propensity to adapt to different surroundings is

one of my greatest strengths. I can always make the best of a bad situation, and over the years I've had to many times. I quickly became part of the furniture in my first year, rising to become Dormitory Captain – which meant it was my responsibility to look after the new boys – and before I knew it I was having the time of my life. There were occasional bouts of homesickness, periods that were very painful to endure, but I doubt there is anyone who has attended a boarding school and not gone through them. We were just children, after all. But your friends pulled you through, so the blues never lasted long. We all developed a great bond of mutual understanding.

Life was organised rigidly, my routine was solid, and as a result I eventually arrived at a lovely feeling of security and warmth. And as for the rules, well, some of them were there to be broken. I became pretty adept at getting up to no good, while making sure I didn't get caught. Perhaps it's in my genes, I don't know, but I found my experiences on the street – or 'street smarts' as I call them – came in handy. It was all pretty innocent – pranks after lights out, slipping out of school at night for fish and chips (a very risky and lucrative enterprise which, if found out, would have resulted in at least a caning from a housemaster).

It was all good training in the art of subterfuge. Kids at boarding schools are just the same as kids anywhere – the moment you're up and about in the morning, you're thinking, What can I get away with? How can I get out of one thing and into another? It's hardly any wonder that public schools are the breeding ground for the nation's finest soldiers, spies and politicians.

The trouble was there was nowhere to hide if you were caught. And I didn't always get away with it. The teachers had seen it all before, and so had the dreaded prefects, and it was these senior boys who tended to dish out a lot of the punishment. The prefects were our Gestapo and, although it was foolish to mess with them, mess with them we did. It was all part of the game. If you stepped out of line you got a beating. The slipper was their favourite. Let me tell you, there's nothing like a size-nine gym shoe to bring a lump to the throat and a tear to the eye. But I never cried. I'd never give them the satisfaction. You had to take it with good grace – thank them even!

One day when I was about eight or nine, I must have been caught in some dastardly misdemeanour and pushed my luck with the prefects more than usual. I'd opened my big mouth in an attempt to lie my way out of it and wound them up big time. Punishment was swift and, as usual, highly imaginative. I'll never forget my two cohorts and I being hauled into a classroom at lunchtime by three big prefects – they were only about 17, but they seemed full-grown men to us. Before we knew it, the bastards had whipped our blazers off, slipped a coat hanger into each, told us to put them back on and then hung us up on coat hooks. Brilliant! There we were, the three of us hanging side by side. To add to it, before long, half the school were pointing through the windows and laughing at us. Oh, the indignity. There was no escape. They left us there the whole of the lunch break. But eventually they came back and let us go. We took it on the chin, of course. There was nothing else you could do. I didn't feel like I'd been abused or anything; we knew we'd done something wrong and we'd been well and truly punished for it. Simple.

The prefects could be ruthless, but when push came to shove the ethos of the school, particularly between the boarders, was 'all for one and one for all'. If a boy needed looking after, everyone would rally around and make sure he was OK. One day I managed to impale my leg on a railing while we were all playing 'run outs' in a part of the school we called the 'bombed gardens' as it had taken a direct hit during the Second World War. I was stuck, in agony, and unable to move. Instead of panicking, all the boys organised themselves immediately. After prising me gently from the railing, they formed a human chain and passed me along. I was so small that they could toss me to one another until I arrived in the arms of a prefect, who whisked me off to the matron. I was bleeding profusely and in shock, but still able to appreciate the gentle efficiency of their actions. It was the quickest way of getting me – one of their own – to safety, and to me it perfectly sums up the wonderful sense of mutual care that permeated the school. That sense of fraternity and camaraderie has never left me and never will. Even today, it is boarding school that I dream of to calm me during times of stress.

'Jamie's academic achievement leaves something to be desired but his sporting abilities are a credit to the school.' So read one of my school reports. I was so proud of the last bit. I loved all the sports at school and I don't think I've ever felt more honoured than when I was named captain of the football, cricket and rugby teams. Dayboys went home to watch television all evening, but for us that was a weekend treat. Us boarders spent all our spare time in the playground squaring up to the older boys. We were super-fit and highly competitive, and sport was everything to us.

Saturday afternoons were the highlight of my week. Chaperoned by my brother Gregory and his friends, we'd head for the Lewisham Odeon or the local ABC cinema. The freedom of being let out for the day, and the magic of watching that week's new release, was heaven. My love of movies began there. *The Italian Job*, *2001: A Space Odyssey*, anything with John Wayne, *Fantasia* and of course each new James Bond – I loved them all.

You can imagine, then, my excitement when I heard that the school was putting on a play. Mr Parry and Mr Nightingale would be holding auditions for their production of *Burke and Hare*. The part I coveted was Jamie the Simpleton – a role I believed was written for me. The teachers didn't disagree either! Mr Parry was a slightly nutty, red-haired, Welsh art teacher (who incidentally appeared in the Richard Burton film version of *Under Milk Wood*) and Mr Nightingale was a lovely New Zealander (who incidentally was the only teacher to get me caned by a headmaster for calling him by his nickname – you guessed it – Florence). Both were wonderful men who were instrumental in encouraging my love of acting. I found the experience so exhilarating and highly addictive. The play was very well received and I remember how proud my mum was of me. Apart from a brief appearance as the Cat in *Peter and the Wolf* at Charles Dickens Primary, this was the beginning of my burgeoning career. I'm still at it over 40 years later, so I must be doing something right.

At the end of each term, my school friends and I parted company. Other boys would return to the four corners of the world – while I would make the short journey back to family and friends in my beloved South London. The contrast between my two worlds could not have been starker. I'd shed my school uniform for civvies and leave the rigidity of rules and regulations behind. Mum and Dad would spoil me rotten – a hint of parental guilt, perhaps? – and I exploited the situation to the full. Having love and goodies heaped on me was wonderful after being away from home for so long.

Dad's exploits allowed him and Mum to enjoy the finer things that Swinging Sixties London had to offer. I remember fantastic lunches at Simpson's in the Strand

and J. Sheekey (Dad's favourite restaurants and still mine today), shopping trips to Harrods and Hamleys and the joys of Carnaby Street in its heyday. We went on fantastic holidays to Portugal, Morocco and once took a stunning trip around Antigua, Jamaica and Nassau in the Bahamas. Wow!

We also owned a caravan at Coghurst in Kent. My aunt Nellie and uncle John would take me down for summer holidays. I adored it. There was a large lake to row and fish in and extensive woodland to explore. Heaven. An added bonus was that most of my dad's friends also had caravans there, which allowed me to spend time with their kids, the Everetts, Masons, Gerrards and O'Maras. To this day, Shelley, Mark and Bradley Everett remain among my closest friends. The dads would come down at weekends and it truly was a magical time.

I loved school and I loved being back at home. I am eternally grateful for having experienced the best of both of those worlds. Mixing with the 'upperworld' and the underworld gave me the ability to be comfortable in any strata of society, and I find I'm never overawed by the company in which I find myself.

Boarding school opened me up to another world. If Mum and Dad hadn't given me that gift, I may have gone down a different path in life. I may have followed in my dad's footsteps far more than I did. Who knows? I may have ended up in a similar position to my beloved father, who in 1968 was charged with the murder of Frank 'The Mad Axeman' Mitchell and with being an accessory in the murder of Jack 'The Hat' McVitie.

I loved living in two worlds. But now, suddenly, my whole life was turned upside down.

3

MURDER?

Mum came and took me out of school to break the news.

'Bad things are going to be said about your father but you mustn't listen to any of them,' she told me, trying to explain what was happening as sympathetically as possible. 'They're accusing him of terrible things and trying to bring him down. But it's all lies. All of it.'

I was completely shocked. A sort of numbness descended on me that makes my memory of the events a little fuzzy. It was all too much to take in. I don't remember the word 'murder' being used around me. After all, it's not the sort of word you use lightly around a ten-year-old, especially in relation to his dad, but I knew that my father was facing life imprisonment and I might lose the man who meant everything to me.

As soon as Dad had been charged, we were surrounded with people who wanted to help and protect us. His network of family, friends, allies and those who owed 'favours' went into full swing. They needed to put their heads together. They needed to get him out of this. In my experience, there really is honour among thieves.

I knew I had to be strong and stand tall for my mum. It's what Dad would have expected. I hated seeing her crying all the time. I wanted to be there for her. But it was decided, rightly, that I should return to school for the time being.

The school's reaction was fantastic. An 'old boy' network similar to ours: 'You always look after your own.' I'll never forget how the headmaster, Mr Furby, sat me down on my return. He was surprisingly gentle and kind, and spoke with reassuring calmness: 'You're not to worry about anything, Jamie. You mustn't talk to anyone outside of school. And don't worry, we're all going to look after you and protect you from this.'

Those words encapsulated the beauty of my boarding school. Whatever was going on, I would not be shunned by the place to which I had grown so attached; nor would I be exposed to the gossip and hearsay that would be circulating in the outside world. I wouldn't be drawn into the chaos surrounding the biggest criminal trial in British legal history to date.

Looking back, it seems incredible that those around me managed to shield me from everything so well, yet they did. We didn't have access to newspapers at school, and I was kept well away from the press who circled the place like vultures. As far as school gossip went, it was 'Woe betide any boy who dares whisper whatever they may hear on the grapevine.' I was safe.

Like I said, the stress the episode placed me under – the way it felt like a surreal, terrible dream – means I can't tell it all exactly as it happened. All I know is that at some point I was back at home before Dad went to trial. The atmosphere at the pub was so different. Dad wasn't there, of course, but the rooms upstairs were constantly buzzing with activity. A lot of my 'uncles' – members of Dad's firm and other associates – were always around. They were there to reassure us, and constantly told us that it was all going to be OK.

They would also huddle in the living room and talk for hours in hushed tones. I wasn't privy to their conversations, but every time I ferried in tea and sandwiches for them I was aware that whatever they were discussing was focused on helping Dad. It wasn't a happy time, but to know that everything possible was being done gave me the focus I needed to stay positive, keep making the tea and feel that I too was doing my bit.

From my experiences at similar meetings later in life – and there have been a few – I know that what seemed mysterious to me then was nothing but my dad's closest, most trusted friends putting their heads together and exploring every possibility on the road to building his defence case. It's quite a formidable thing to witness men who plan crimes with professional precision employing the same attention to detail when trying to get out of them. The atmosphere of intensity and focus is something to behold.

The first charge Dad faced was for the murder of Frank Mitchell. Mitchell was known as 'The Mad Axeman' – you don't get a nickname like that for nothing, do you? Anyway, the charge came about on the evidence of a man called Albert Donahue, who claimed he was an eyewitness to Mitchell's shooting. Donahue was one of the Kray firm who'd turned supergrass and gave evidence for the prosecution. Perhaps he had his reasons, but Donahue broke one of the fundamental rules of the underworld – never grass. Once you cross that line, you never live it down. The act of snitching comes to define you in the eyes of many. Including yours truly. Donahue is the lowest of the low. He'll never escape it and he will die a grass.

Yet Donahue's uncorroborated testimony didn't get the result he and the authorities were after. Dad was found not guilty. He'd avoided the biggie – a life sentence. It was no time to celebrate, though. Once he had been acquitted of murder, Dad had to face the charge of being an accessory in the murder of Jack

McVitie. Jack 'The Hat' was an associate of the Krays
who, like Mitchell, had become a liability to them. The
Krays had killed him, and my father was accused of
disposing of the body.

4

GUILTY

I can't recall the moment when I learned my dad had been found guilty. Perhaps I didn't know what 'accessory to murder' meant – perhaps I didn't want to know – but what I did know was that Dad had been found guilty of that charge. He had been taken away and wouldn't be back for a very long time. The sentence was ten years – as long as I'd been alive. I was devastated.

Mum had held it together for so long, but once Dad was sentenced she went to pieces for a while. She took to her room for days, and kept the lights off. The atmosphere in the pub was dead and a sort of silence descended on our lives. Mum couldn't face anyone. I didn't feel much like it either.

The news was a total bombshell, but young as I was

I knew I had to protect myself so that I could be there for Mum. I didn't go into denial about what was happening, but I did my best not to let the pain get hold of me. I had to shield myself from my own emotions and be strong. When I look back at the little boy I was, I've got a lot of respect for him. He took on a lot and coped with a lot and I don't know how he did it, I really don't.

A man's prison sentence is also a sentence on his family, and it's always devastating, especially at first. There wasn't a lot I could do for Mum apart from just be there for her, bring her cups of coffee, tell her I love her, and let her know it was OK to be upset. Sure enough, Mum slowly came round. She was dealing with something momentous, and she dealt with it well. When the chips are down, my mum's a very strong woman.

I hadn't spent time with Dad for a long while – ever since he had been arrested – and I was absolutely desperate to see him. But my mum told me that we would have to wait as people who received long sentences weren't allowed visits straight away. Eventually, the chance came to visit Dad in Leicester Prison.

I'd never been to Leicester before. We arrived on a foggy winter's day and the place was a shock, to put it mildly. It looked like a horrible city, or at least that's how it seemed to me, if only because I knew that my father was incarcerated there. I'll never forget how cold it was the day me and Mum first set eyes on the jail, which sits on a big, bleak common. I remember thinking it looked like a medieval castle.

We were taken through the huge wooden gates and ushered into a waiting room. Suddenly we were in a different world. A world of slamming doors, of echoes, the sound of men's voices filling the hallways, the clanging of metal on metal. It was my first time inside a prison and it was even more horrible than I expected. I'd never seen so many uniforms and sets of keys in one place. The screws had a terrible habit of swinging their great big bunches of keys in a way that was both menacing and annoying.

I took it all in as we were processed, then taken through door after door, and all the time there was a knot in my stomach. I just wanted to see my dad, but first we had to wait. The feeling of being in that waiting room that day will never leave me. Immediately I became aware of other visitors looking at us and whispering. They knew who we were, and why we were there. Once again it struck me what a reputation Dad had.

They could whisper all they wanted, it didn't bother me. Mum looked so beautiful – dressed immaculately as always, wearing her best jewellery. I felt so proud to be next to her, her head held high and me on my best behaviour. We waited in one corner of the room until a prison guard told everyone to move to another door. 'Could you just wait here, Mrs Foreman,' he said as everybody else filed out.

It looked as if we were getting special treatment, but there was nothing special about it – we had to wait because we were destined for a different part of the prison. After a few minutes, we were taken off through another set of gates that led into the main yard. I looked up and saw this dark tower – it looked like a castle within a castle – surrounded by an empty moat. It was daunting, ominous and obviously special. Dad was being kept in an inner sanctum, I thought. I was right. At the time it was the highest-security prison unit in England.

We moved towards the building, following a guard. We descended a stone staircase. It was as if we were heading to the dungeons. The guard tapped on a door and a hatch slid open. Two eyes – another screw. The door unlocked and swung open. We passed through and the door slammed shut behind us. The new screw ushered us down a long corridor to another door. Another hatch. More eyes. Countless doors, countless corridors. Hatch after hatch, screw after screw, it seemed endless. What *is* this place? I thought. I felt like we were descending into hell or something, travelling towards a dark place a million miles from the outside world. Was my dad *really* in here somewhere?

Then, suddenly, we walked through a door into a carpeted room with no windows. As I entered I saw two screws sitting behind a desk. I looked around the room, and there he was.

My dad.

Arms wide open and a big smile on his face, he was beaming: 'Well, come here and give us a cuddle then.'

I rushed into his arms. It was absolutely glorious. Being with Dad again was like reaching the promised land after floundering so long in the wilderness. We all forgot about the depressing surroundings because Dad looked so strong, so *normal*, that he made me feel nothing but happiness.

'This is how it is going to be, Jamie,' he said, gesturing to our surroundings, 'but it doesn't matter to us as long as we make the most of this time together.' Beautiful words I'll never forget.

It was a wonderful visit. Dad was Dad, exactly as he'd always been. Circumstances had changed, but he didn't seem fazed by any of it. During those moments, seeing my father being so strong for us, I felt such respect and awe for him. His dignity was something to aspire to.

There was so much love in that room I could have stayed there with him for all eternity. But we were soon reminded that only one person would be staying. Hearing 'time's up' was like a punch in the stomach, but Dad was ready to buoy us up a little. 'Everything's going to be all right,' he said, holding me tight. 'You'll see me again soon. And look after your mother for me.'

I knew I had to be strong, and I had to believe in the future. If Dad could do it, I could too. To him prison was the price you pay for living the life he led – if you can't do the time...

I was his son. In many ways I had benefited from the things he had done and now things were difficult I was prepared to suffer the consequences with him.

Saying goodbye was awful, though 'awful' is hardly the word. It was heartbreaking. Worse still was all those doors slamming shut behind us – another sharp reminder of where we were and that my dad had been snatched away from me. It hit me like a ton of bricks. An hour earlier I'd walked down the same corridors and through the same doors, yet I'd been heading somewhere I wanted to go. Now I was going through the same, painfully slow process, but I was being dragged away. Each slamming door confirmed I was getting further away from who I wanted to be with.

Once outside, I didn't look back. There was no point. All I wanted to do was get away from the prison, away from grey, horrible Leicester and back to London. A cab took us to the station and we boarded the train. Leaving my dad behind in that place was the hardest thing I have ever had to do. It made me feel somehow guilty. I felt like I was deserting him. That painful memory has stayed with me all my life.

Mum always gave us a treat after our visits. Once back in London, she'd help revive my flagging spirits and help me wash away some of the pain I felt leaving Dad. 'Let's go out for dinner,' she would say, and then take me to this lovely Italian place in the Strand, or to the Spaghetti

House. I'll always love her for that, and for the strength she showed in those moments when she realised the pain of not having Dad around was overwhelming me.

Coming to terms with Dad being away was a journey that took quite some time. There were always little reminders that he wasn't around, and each one made the situation feel sadder. You always tried to stay positive, and always held on to the promise that it wasn't going be this way for ever, but some moments really brought home the nightmare of the whole thing.

Before he went away, Dad always used to come and pick me up from school for the holidays. He never missed one end of term. I remember standing at the dorm window and looking out across Blackheath until I spotted his car, a beautiful postbox-red Mercedes 220SE. It was a real tool, that car – beautiful black leather seats, chrome hubs, eight-track stereo, tail wings at the back – and I loved watching it arc over the hill and down towards me.

It was Christmas, and the first end of term since Dad had been locked up. My uncle John Fitzgerald, Nellie's husband, was due to pick me up. I was fine with that, but what I didn't know was that he'd be driving Dad's red Mercedes. Much as I loved my uncle Fitzy, it was a tough pill to swallow seeing that car speed towards the school without my dad at the wheel.

Until that moment it hadn't quite hit me that my dad wasn't going to come back to us for a long, long time. A few months had already felt like an age, but it hurt seeing that wonderful car again and knowing I'd be able to drive it myself by the time Dad became a free man again. A sense of how long ten years really was began to dawn on me, and it was nauseating. The previous Christmas, Dad had whisked me and the family off to the Bahamas. This Christmas was going to be the worst we ever had. The first of many hollow, empty holidays. How times had changed.

And how times *were* changing. Going home wasn't the same any more. The pub was still busy – business was even brisker for a while, thanks to a bit of post-trial notoriety – and our family was surrounded by good people who rallied around and looked after us. It helped, of course, but Dad had been such a momentous presence that his absence was always gnawing away.

Nobody's life got easier once Dad went away. It was the end of an era for many of his firm as well. It was as if they'd all run out of time. So many were nicked for one thing or another. The sixties had been a momentous, special time for them, then suddenly it all felt like it was over and everything seemed miserable.

Yet, despite everything, I was holding it together. So far.

5

IN PIECES AND BACK TOGETHER

There was a German with a bomb and he was waiting to jump out and kill me. I was convinced of it. He was hiding behind a lorry near the pub. In a few seconds, I was going to be blown to smithereens. I couldn't move – fear had rooted me to the spot – and, boy, did I need to get out of there. But it was no good: I was stuck. Panic gripped me and I began to scream, and as I screamed I found I could run, but instead of retreating I leaped forwards and dashed past the lorry towards the pub. Yelling, I collapsed at the door.

A couple of regulars scooped me up and took me inside to safety. My mum was beside herself. 'Where have you been, Jamie? What's happened to you?'

I didn't have an answer. I was delirious, deranged even. There'd been a German outside, I'd panicked and now I was in the pub wearing my pyjamas and crying with confusion and fear. That was all I knew.

The episode was a bit of a mystery. I'd been outside, that's for sure, but there had been no German, and there was no explanation as to how and why I was out on the street in my pyjamas. Minutes before everything went off, I'd been snuggled up in a chair watching a war documentary on telly in the lounge above the pub, and I remember I had a bit of flu coming on. Next thing I knew, I was a block or two away from the pub, waiting for the traffic on Marshalsea Road to pass so I could cross and get home. Then I'd seen the lorry and wound up in a terrible state.

The weird thing is, nobody could work out how I'd managed to leave the pub unnoticed. There was no way I could have gone through the bar without raising eyebrows. The only likely explanation was that I'd fallen asleep and then somehow dropped myself out of the first-floor window. If that's what happened, never mind the German: I was lucky I hadn't done myself some serious damage.

The family doctor, Leo Barry, was called. I can't remember what he asked me, but I now know that during his hushed conversation with Mum he told her he thought I was having a bit of a breakdown. Things had obviously got to me, he said, and what I needed was some rest and a bit of TLC. Looking back, I can see how right he was.

Around the time of this incident, my mum had started to really get herself together, and I'd been so relieved to see her getting back to somewhere near her best again. Her condition had been very, very worrying. I felt such admiration for her – to go through what she'd gone through and to come out the other side had required real strength. I'd done as much as I could to support her, and now that the pressure was off a little I was left with feelings I'd put aside for Mum and Danielle's sake.

Confusing states of sadness and anger left me pretty emotionally vulnerable, I suppose, and in the end I wasn't equipped to deal with them at my age. It was as if I'd been in an emotional strait-jacket until that night, and the delirium outside the pub was my feelings wrestling free. My safety valve blew and I was left in a tangle of upset about everything that we'd been through after losing Dad.

Mum followed the doctor's orders, making sure I got the rest and care I needed. I was off school for a while and I remember spending a lot of time just crying and crying. Letting it all out was a positive thing, a cathartic process that did me a lot of good. For so long I'd hindered my acceptance of the situation by trying to stay strong, but now it was time to cut myself some slack and allow myself a bit of natural, human weakness. It was a case of having to hit rock bottom before picking yourself up and *really* taking control of things.

My dad was gone, but he *was* coming back. That was the thing I needed to keep hold of – I had to accept a positive and a negative at the same time. I'd get to see him on visits, but otherwise I just had to get on with it. End of story.

School had always been a constant in my life, but as time went on I started to go off it. I'd been growing up pretty fast and it became increasingly hard to see the point in studying when I had so much else on my mind. 'Just getting on with it' was all very well, but when I was around 13 I realised school was no longer much of a priority for a number of reasons. For starters, I was no longer a boarder. I'd become a dayboy so I could be around for Mum a lot more, but the change meant I no longer felt part of the school's team spirit. It was all a bit depressing; my heart simply wasn't in it any more.

Things weren't looking too rosy outside school either. The sixties had been an amazing decade. Everybody had money in their pockets and the good times had rolled in our pub and elsewhere besides. But, as the seventies loomed, all that *joie de vivre* started to slip away. In its place you suddenly had the three-day week and a feeling of austerity everywhere. Maybe it's just me, but it felt like everything changed almost in the blink of an eye. Where you'd once had a world exploding with colour and noise, you now had one filled with darkness and gloom.

Slowly but surely business dropped off at the pub until it wasn't the same place any more. Gone were the days of players and pretty ladies filling its four walls on a Friday. There were some nights where it just felt dead, with Dad's jukebox playing to just a couple of regulars. And the deader our beloved little pub got, the more we were reminded of the good times with Dad. Happy memories that also made us sad.

Nostalgia's all well and good, but Mum didn't want to hold on to a business for the sake of it. Financially it wasn't making sense, so we took the hard decision to sell up. We needed a clean break, not so we could forget Dad, but so we could stay focused on building a future with him when he got out. It would be sad to say goodbye to the place, but a relief at the same time. You can't hold on to anything for ever.

The pub sold quick enough. It was time to move and, thanks to Dad, we had somewhere to go. Before he went away, he had invested in a beautiful five-bedroom house in Red Post Hill, Dulwich, and now it was to be our home. We moved in and it felt good to be in a new place where we could give attention to each other as a family without the worries of running a business. There was the inevitable financial pinch of Dad no longer bringing in money, but, although times were lean, we had each other, and that's all that mattered.

My routine didn't change much after our move, but Mum soon sensed my lack of enthusiasm for being a dayboy at Christ's College. She was willing to take the strain of finding the money for my school fees, but only if I could look her in the eye and say it was worth the trouble. Christ's College had been a true education, and the school was so helpful and supportive of me through everything that had happened with Dad. Still, I'd simply lost interest, and had also been bunking off, so I made the decision to leave the school that had meant so much to me. It was time to go. A time for new beginnings.

It was suggested that I go to the local comprehensive in Dulwich, but there was no way I was going to do that. It sounds terrible, but I didn't like the look of the kids I saw coming in and out of the place. Me, a working-class kid, had turned into a right little snob. The fact that they didn't do the sports I was into was also a real turn-off. I was 14 years old, I'd been through a fuck of a lot and quite simply I didn't think I had much to gain from the place. So I decided to take my chances, bide my time and see what life might have to offer elsewhere.

After I quit school I spent a lot of time being the man of the house, helping Mum out with this and that and taking my sister to school. Once I'd dropped Danielle off at Dulwich Hamlet Primary each morning, I suddenly found I had a lot of time on my hands. I'd hang about and my mind would wander. I'd daydream about what I might start doing for a living, but I'd daydream more about my dad.

The more I thought about him, the more I started to wonder just who Freddie Foreman was. I'd heard rumours about what went down, whisperings about what kind of a man my father was when he wasn't being a father, but I'd spent so many years being protected from the details. Now I was a teenager, my mind became more curious to know the truth, *whatever* it was.

One day I decided to start finding out, so I went to Brixton Library to do a bit of detective work.

From the moment Dad had been arrested, I'd been told many things by many people: Freddie Foreman was innocent, he'd been fitted up, the authorities had been trying to bring him down for years and finally they'd managed it. I believed what I was told – I heard it all from my nearest and dearest and had no reason to doubt them. Not until I started sniffing around in the library, that is. What I discovered changed everything.

According to the newspapers, my dad was a 'monster', as guilty as sin. At the library, I spent hour after hour poring over acres of newspaper reports kept on microfilm, reading anything pertaining to him. If I'd ever had any doubts about whether my dad was innocent or guilty, well, just taking in what they said about him put them to bed. I sat there in awe of what I was reading; it was nothing short of a revelation. My dad was a South

London gangland boss. A killer at the centre of the most powerful crime organisation in Britain. He was accused of being the 'Man Who Held The Key' in some of the Kray twins' most nefarious deeds. Fucking hell! I knew my dad was a 'face', sure, but until then I'd had no idea how *massively* he had been involved in the whole thing. The way the papers put it, he sounded less like *my* father and more like the *God*father. He was Britain's Al Capone.

As I devoured every column inch available, the picture of him grew bigger and bigger. Dad's trial had been part of a huge showdown between the establishment, the police and the Krays, and at the time it was the longest trial in British criminal history. It ended in my father being convicted of disposing of Jack 'The Hat' McVitie's body. That was the 'accessory to murder' bit. Jack was a troublesome member of the twins' firm who was brutally stabbed to death by Reggie Kray.

The papers were certainly right about Dad knowing the Krays – I vividly remembered Ronnie and Reggie babysitting me when I was small. From time to time Dad had left me with them at their East End snooker hall when he had business over that way. They were always so lovely to me, and made sure I was well looked after. That was my experience of them, but I didn't need Brixton Library to tell me the Krays weren't angels to everyone.

Everyone knew the twins were notorious criminals,

but if you were on the right side of them you were all right. Being who I was meant I certainly was. To my dad they were allies and friends. Dad was very much his own man, but he'd helped the twins on occasion, mainly out of loyalty to one of his best friends, Charlie Kray. Charlie was a lovely, lovely man. He certainly didn't have the same dark, dangerous nature of his brothers. Anybody who knew him will tell you that. Nevertheless, he was unjustly tarred with the same brush. I am proud to have had the honour of reading the eulogy at his funeral. I loved Charlie and miss him very much.

After years of being kept in the dark, I suddenly had the whole picture of who my dad was, how he was perceived by the public and what he had done. Technically speaking, I'd been lied to by those close to me. Dad wasn't innocent; he hadn't been fitted up. He had done some terrible things, and that was that. But I wasn't angry about the lies, because right away I understood that the truth had been kept from me for my own protection. Those 'lies' were born out of love. At the age of ten there's no way I could have dealt with the facts I was now facing at 14. No way at all. God knows how that little boy would have reacted to the truth about his father.

But how did that boy react at 14? Did he feel angry, ashamed, all messed up? Was he thrown into a terrible dilemma? Did he hate his father for the things he'd done, for the fact that he'd put himself in a position where he had been labelled a 'monster'?

Not guilty, dear reader. Not guilty.

My father wasn't just the man I thought he was – a good, loving father. In my young eyes, what I'd found out made Dad more of a man than I'd thought he was. I already had so much adoration for my dad and, if I'm honest, discovering how notorious he was only strengthened that feeling. The press might have condemned Freddie Foreman's actions, but there's no denying that they created a certain mystique around him. Whatever villainy he'd been up to, my dad was presented as a hugely powerful figure at the top of his game, a man both revered and feared in many echelons of society.

The public has always been obsessed with criminals – gangsters in particular – and rightly or wrongly the baddies have been romanticised in films and literature since time immemorial. They go from villains to heroes to legends. Perhaps there's a part in all of us that lives out deeply hidden dreams of power and lawlessness through such characters, I don't know. At 14, I'd seen plenty of gangster films, and to discover that my dad was the real deal undoubtedly gave me a buzz. When it comes to that 14-year-old boy, I think he was rather glad his dad was a man at the top of his particular tree.

But my reaction was more complex than a schoolboy

fantasy come true. I suppose some might say I had two choices: I could either demonise Dad for who and what he was, or I could idolise him. Well, if it was one or the other, there was no way I was going to write my own dad off as an evil man. In fact, it didn't even occur to me that he was anything of the sort. To demonise a man who had never shown me anything but love and kindness would have been absurd. Besides, I understood that, in the world my father moved in, certain deeds went with the territory. There were men out there who he might have hurt – killed even – but those men would have just as happily got him first.

As far as Dad's guilt went, perversely I wanted to believe he was guilty. It helped me. To see my own dad suffering for years in prison, to feel my mother's and sister's pain, and to deal with my own demons would have been so much harder had I genuinely believed he was innocent. If he was guilty, at least there was some reason for all this misery.

And it had been misery. Not that I blamed Dad. He did what he had to do and was willing to pay the price. The rules of his world. My dad was my hero, no matter what he'd done. In his absence, I loved him more than ever and was willing to pay *my* price for him not being around. Perhaps I even romanticised him a touch too much – nobody's perfect, after all. But back then, with Dad away, all I had to go on were my memories of his strength and kindness during those visits, and the wonderful stories I was told about him, his loyalty to his friends, the people he had helped over the years. Dad was larger than life to me and I adored him all the more for it.

It always astounded me when I heard other kids badmouthing their parents. To hear one of my mates say, 'I hate my dad' baffled me. How could you? I'd think. For one, I couldn't relate to having anything to hate a parent for, and secondly it made me mad seeing other kids take for granted what I craved so much: a father, at home, where he should be. See how you hate your dad when he's snatched from you and thrown in jail, I'd think.

I didn't blame Dad for anything, but I was still angry that he wasn't in my life. My discoveries at the library did lessen the pain, if only a little − at least I was no longer in the dark about why my father had been taken away from me − but, like anyone who's angry, I looked for a scapegoat. If my father wasn't to blame, someone was. And in my mind that someone turned out to be two 'someones': the Kray twins.

The more I read about the twins, and the more I spoke to my parents' friends about Dad's relationship with them, the more I came to think it was their fault that my dad was in prison. For years Ronnie and Reggie had run the East End of London, and there's no doubt they were powerful men whose influence went deep. They made a lot of money and for quite a while did it without drawing attention to themselves. Then things started to go wrong.

Bit by bit they started to lose the plot. Some people reckon it was their public profile and taste for celebrity status, others blame Ronnie's ego and increasingly unstable mind, but for one reason or another the twins began to run amok and stopped covering their tracks. It was like they just wanted people to know what they were all about, and all professional caution went out the window. They were shooting people in broad daylight, for fuck's sake, making a completely unnecessary name for themselves. But that was up to them. The problem was, they dragged my dad's name along with them.

As I said, Dad was never part of their 'firm', but he was associated with it. The twins had done him good turns, put him on to some good touches, and out of loyalty my dad did what he felt was right: he stuck by them. Others turned their backs on the twins to save themselves, and I know that people who loved my dad had urged him to distance himself from them. But Dad's sense of duty to return a favour was too strong. Unfortunately, his sense of honour was his downfall.

I took this information and ran with it. As far as I was concerned, it was the twins' fault for taking liberties with my dad's loyalty and getting him in too deep. Through their sloppy, unnecessary actions, I felt they'd stuck it on my dad. The very mention of the Krays would make me livid, and my mum too. It was a very sore point for a very long time.

The truth is, I cherry-picked the negative comments I heard about the Krays so I could weave a protective web around my father. The Krays were my scapegoat for some time, but over the years I came to realise that I was wrong to blame them for Dad's actions. Call it six of one, half a dozen of the other, the truth is my dad did what he did and no one made him do it. But still, I could never be angry with my hero.

Never.

It was around this time that Dad was moved from Leicester Prison to Wormwood Scrubs. Mum had relentlessly campaigned for him to be relocated nearer to London, bombarding the Home Office with letters, and eventually it paid off. Dad had been very much alone up in Leicester, and the strain of those visits had been getting to all of us. Having Dad closer to home was a godsend. He was still locked up, yes, but in the Scrubs he was suddenly around men he knew and trusted. Men he went a long way back with. A lot of the Great Train Robbery chaps were in there – my godfather Buster Edwards, Gordon Goody, Jimmy Hussey, and other old friends Billy Gentry, Roy Hilder and Alan Gold. The other prisoners called them the LGs – London Gangsters. Knowing Dad was in good company eased our minds a lot, and visits became a lot less painful. Going to Leicester had always been a long, miserable journey, and now we only needed to travel across town to White City to see Dad among his friends.

Perversely, I have some pretty fond memories of visiting Dad at the Scrubs. He was still a Category A prisoner held in D Wing, but he and the chaps all worked in the laundry, so whenever we saw them they always looked smart, even in their prison uniforms, which they made sure were clean and pressed. Seeing my dad make the best of a bad situation, and managing to look smart and respectable even in Her Majesty's denim trousers and shirts with wide stripes, made a lasting impression on me. Dad always had his head held high, was always clean shaven and neatly coiffured, and it said a lot about his strength of character.

I'll always remember Dad walking into the visiting room, stopping to hold his arms out while the screws rubbed him down, and acting as though it was all so normal. He never let the bastards get him down, and would look over to us and wink and grin. He looked so strong and in control, no matter what the circumstances. I've taken that example and always tried to be the same in front of my sons.

Mum and I used to make a packed lunch for every visit on the premise that it was a long day for me and I had to have something to eat. But it was really for Dad. We took smoked-salmon sandwiches, on brown bread of course – Dad's nickname is Brown Bread Fred – sweet and sour dill pickles and a prawn cocktail in a flask cup.

The flask itself was filled with a good dry white wine. The wives and friends of the other chaps would all do the same, including my darling godmother June. She and Mum have been great friends since they were young and always laughed and giggled together. They still do today.

We'd always sit at the back of the visiting room. None of the other prisoners would occupy those tables. It seemed as if they were reserved just for us. The screws never bothered us, even when someone dropped their flask one day and the contents – gin – spilled all over the floor. It smelled like a distillery, yet they turned a blind eye. These men had a lot of influence over the smooth running of the nick, and if they kept certain prisoners sweet it was easier all round.

It was marvellous seeing the chaps together with their wives all dressed up, wearing their best jewellery and looking lovely, and most of the screws were very polite to us during our visits. They'd exchange pleasantries with us, ask us how we were and say how nice it was to see us again. Those guards were no trouble, and once the visit began they just kept an eye out from a distance, knowing there'd be no grief if the chaps were given a bit of leeway. Sometimes we'd be having such a good time that it felt more like a social occasion than a prison visit, and that was partly down to decent screws cutting everyone some slack. But there was one screw I'll never forget.

I had never seen him before. When Mum and I handed

him our visiting order, he just growled at us to take a seat. I took an instant dislike to him for being so rude to my mother. The screw was a big lump with a surly manner, a right miserable bastard straight out of a Dickens novel. He sat at a big wooden lectern – a reading chair with a desk attached – which was raised up so he could look over the whole room. Still, we had better things to worry about and never gave the bloke the time of day.

On this occasion we were with one of my dad's oldest friends, Ronnie Oliffe. Ron and my dad go back a long way. He was always my father's wing man in his clubs and pubs. Whenever there was any trouble and Dad 'went to work', meaning got into a fight, Ron was always at his shoulder. They had never lost a fight. There are some legendary stories about how, with just their hands, they've left five or six big lumps spark out. Years later I saw them in action with my own eyes, and everything I'd ever heard was true, believe me. A real dynamic duo.

It had been a lovely visit, as always. We were sitting around, and knew time was nearly up. Just as we were getting around to goodbyes, the screw from the lectern waltzed over and banged his hand down on to the table. 'Time!' he shouted, his hand pressed on the tabletop.

Dad didn't look up, but nonchalantly moved his eyes to the screw's hand. 'All right, guv'nor,' said Dad, his voice steady, quiet and cold.

The screw walked back to his perch in the corner.

Calmly, Dad looked across to Ronnie. They held each

other's gaze a few seconds, and in those moments there was a flicker of electricity between them. Neither of them said a word, but there was the subtlest change in atmosphere around the table, an eerie calm. I didn't know what this meant, but Mum did, it seemed. 'Fred,' she said, looking worried. 'Don't you…'

'Don't worry, it's all right,' he said, still calm, still measured.

Time was well and truly up now. All the other visitors had filed out of the room. It was just us and the rest of the screws, but Dad didn't move a muscle. Sure enough, the same screw started walking towards us again.

'We should go,' said Mum, gathering up the flask and lunchboxes.

'Just stay there,' said Dad. 'No need to go just yet.'

'I told you. Time!' said the screw, his hand coming down on the table three times. Bang, bang, bang.

Dad ignored him and smiled at me. 'Come here and give me a little cuddle,' he said. I smiled back.

'I thought I told you, Foreman,' shouted the screw, his face reddening. 'Time!'

'I told you, I'm coming,' said Dad, calm as anything. He didn't raise his voice one bit. 'Come on, time to go,' he added, smiling at us.

We stood up and moved towards the door, Dad with his arms on my shoulders. We got outside, and Dad gave Mum a kiss and a hug. The same routine as always, yet something felt strange. It was as if Dad was a little bit removed from the situation, like there was something else on his mind as he went through the motions of saying goodbye. In the middle of whatever we were saying, Dad broke off suddenly.

'Hang on,' he said quietly, 'I won't be a second.'

With that, he walked back into the visiting room. Mum looked a bit alarmed, so Ronnie took her arm a second and smiled. 'Don't worry,' he said. Then he went after Dad.

Ronnie must have known something I didn't. All I knew was Mum looked worried and Dad was back in the visiting room for some reason. I walked over to the door and peered into the room. On one side there were three or four wardens. Ron was looking at them but they all seemed to be looking the other way. I'll never forget the scene that met my eyes.

Dad had gone to the front of the lectern, grabbed the guard by his collar and dragged him across the desk with one arm until their faces were level. The cocky bastard who, moments ago, had been banging his fist and barking orders was now hanging over his desk, my dad's finger in his face, and begging for mercy.

'I'm sorry, Foreman, I'm sorry,' he pleaded, his arms flailing around while Dad quietly laid down the law.

I crept forward enough to hear my dad saying, 'If you ever talk to me like that in front of my family again, I'll break your fucking jaw.'

Even I felt a cold shiver run down my spine.

'I'm apologising, I'm sorry,' the screw kept repeating. He looked petrified, desperate to calm my dad down.

Perhaps the other screws thought Dad had a point and that the screw had what was coming to him, or were scared of interfering with my dad in full flow – maybe both – for they did nothing to try to stop what was happening. Even so, Ronnie was there to mind my dad's back. They all just looked the other way as Dad seemed about to go to work.

I was transfixed, my mouth agape at the scene. I'd never seen Dad really lose it before, and it was an awesome spectacle. I was frozen, fascinated, shocked and proud, all at the same time. I wondered if Dad was about to take things further. Was he about to lay this odious, objectionable man out?

The answer was no, thankfully. After a few more strong words, Dad threw the bloke back into his chair as easily as you'd brush off a fly, then calmly walked back to where I was waiting. I took one more look at the screw slumped in his chair. He was a different man. Instead of pulling him from his perch to the floor, Dad had dragged him over it, bringing their eyes to the same level, literally showing the screw that he could not talk down to my dad. Then, when done, he'd shoved him back up to his position of authority and made a mockery of it. Before, the screw had been puffed up with self-importance and power, above us all at his lectern. Now he looked weak, defeated. Pathetic. It was the last time I ever saw him. On our next visit a new – very polite – guard was sitting at the lectern.

Then Dad was back with us, breathing just a little harder and licking his slightly curled lips. I would see that face many times again over the years, but it was that day I learned to read the signs.

After a couple of minutes, Dad cracked a smile and gave us a hug. The storm had passed.

'Just like the old days, Freddie,' smiled Ronnie, and they had a bit of a giggle about it. Ronnie would not have hesitated in risking getting nicked to help my dad. The sense of loyalty my father commanded was earned because he had shown the same to his friends all his life. It was and is an unimpeachable code of honour.

'I'm going to have murders over him,' said Dad with a grin. 'Still...'

I'd read about my dad's reputation, and now I'd been given a taste of how powerful he could be, and how suddenly he could switch from one mood to another. There had been no screaming and shouting, just a steely determination to take it to the edge. Dad would never let anyone disrespect him or his family. The more I came to understand my father, the more I loved him, and the more I could believe things were OK for him in prison. There was light at the end of the tunnel.

I had been in pieces, but slowly I was getting back together. My dad had made his decisions in life, and now I had some decisions of my own to make.

By now I'd been out of school for a good year and I was staring my 15th birthday in the face. I'd knocked about here and there, revisiting old mates in the Borough, I'd been down the library and looked after the house, but I was getting bored. I didn't want to go back to school, but I knew I needed to find something to occupy my days. Mum agreed.

'You can't just do nothing,' she said one day. 'I feel terrible you're not at school, and I'm not going to let you waste yourself.'

Thank God for those words. It wasn't that I was wasting my life, but she was right. If she hadn't made me have a good think, I may well have ambled along as I was for a good few years, or maybe the authorities would have caught up with me and made me go to school. Who knows? Anyway, Mum was the catalyst I needed to help me take control of my destiny.

During my time at home, I'd been watching a lot of telly, and good telly at that. It was the early seventies, and at that time British drama was at its best. We had the greatest writers in the world writing plays that were shown weekly on the BBC – earth-shatteringly brilliant people like Dennis Potter, Alan Sillitoe and Alan Plater were giving the nation programmes to really get their teeth into, and I remember being glued to every *Play For Today*, among other fantastic dramas.

I was still an avid cinema-goer too, and ended up spending a lot of my time thinking about the other worlds I encountered at the pictures or on the box. I suppose it made me a bit of a dreamer, which meant I was never bored. As I started to wonder what I could do with myself, I began to dream that I could do what all those people I took such pleasure in watching did: acting.

6

A NEW DIRECTION

Mum spoke first. 'Jamie's got something to ask you,' she said to Dad. 'He wants to talk to you about something.'

'Oh,' said Dad, raising an eyebrow. 'What's that then?'

We were at the end of a visit, and I'd spent the whole time waiting to get something off my chest.

'I want to be an actor, Dad,' I said brightly. 'I want to go to acting school.'

There was a pause. Dad looked down and licked his lips, and for a second I wondered what he was thinking. After all, my news was a bit out of the blue. I smiled and shifted in my seat, trying to gauge his reaction. The wheels were certainly turning in his head, but I didn't know what he was thinking.

'Now this is what you do,' said Dad, looking at Mum. 'Go to Ronnie Knight and get a message to Barbara. Tell Ronnie what Jamie wants to do and see if there's anything she can do for him.'

Mum nodded and smiled at me. Ronnie Knight and my uncle Mick Regan owned the A & R, a drinking club in Charing Cross Road, and his wife Barbara wasn't just any Barbara: she was Barbara Windsor, belle of the *Carry On* films and one of Britain's most famous actresses. Good old Dad, he'd come up with a fantastic idea, just like that. I was so happy and excited. He looked at me, smiling. With his blessing and support, I suddenly felt what could have easily remained a pipedream might actually become a reality.

'If Barbara can't help you, then I'll have another think,' Dad added. 'But try her first and let's see. So what's made you choose acting anyway?'

Good question. Looking back, it's so touching that Dad came up with a plan to help me into acting before he even asked why. It's just as well, because my answer was a touch flimsy.

'I don't know,' I said quite honestly. 'I've been out of school for a while now. I need some direction. I love films and I just thought I'd like to give it a try.'

'Good,' beamed Dad. 'Fantastic. Let's see what happens then, eh?'

I grinned. There was no doubt in his voice, no hint of disapproval, no attempt to sound me out. If it was what

I wanted, he and Mum were right behind me, and I couldn't have wished for a more encouraging response. I look back on that visit as the most pivotal moment in my life. A conversation that most families have around a dining table, we had in a visiting room in Wormwood Scrubs Prison. Somehow the scene sums up my life at that time – we never seemed to go about anything the way normal families did.

I'll never forget being next to Mum as she put down the receiver after talking to Ronnie Knight. I was so excited I could barely contain myself.

'What did he say, what did he say?' I asked.

Mum smiled. 'He said he's going to talk to Barbara and see what she can do.'

Music to my ears. I hugged her. But, as always, Mum kept my feet firmly on the ground. 'Remember, it's a hard business, Jamie. Don't get too excited ... not just yet.'

I didn't have time to get too excited, as the next thing we knew Barbara Windsor was on the phone. I'd met Barbara when I was younger, and speaking to her again was simply lovely. What a wonderful lady.

'All right, babe,' Barbara started. 'So you want to be an actor? Listen, why don't you come over to see me?'

At that point Barbara was in a pantomime at the Odeon Theatre at Temple Fortune, near Golders Green, and she told me to get the bus up and pay her a visit before one of the performances. Filled with expectation, I put my best suit on – a smart, navy-blue, three-piece chalkstripe I'd bought in Guvnor's on the Walworth Road – and my beautiful sheepskin coat. The journey was interminable. I got the 'Undie' from Brixton to Golders Green and then took a bus to the theatre, a route worked out for me by Barbara. Then I reported to my first stage door and was shown to her dressing room.

'Hello, my darling,' said Barbara, bubbly and kind as ever. 'Come in and sit yourself down. I'm just getting ready for the show.'

It was magic being a 15-year-old kid from South London and sitting backstage surrounded by all the accoutrements of the acting profession – the dressing-room mirror framed with lights; the wigs; the make-up; the cards from fans. It looked straight out of a movie. Added to that, the smell of the greasepaint well and truly got its hooks into me. As I sat there with Barbara, the other actors began to trickle in.

The room buzzed as everyone said hello and began to get ready. I'd never been backstage at a theatre before, or felt the sense of anticipation that builds in the room before a performance, but I was feeling it now. Big time. It all felt so ordinary, yet extraordinary too.

Busy though she was, Barbara chatted away while I watched her get ready for the panto, and took the time to introduce me to everyone in the show, including the DJ Ed Stewart. Wow, I thought, it's Ed Stewart from *Crackerjack*, the kids' TV show! I also met Annie Ross, the great jazz singer. Impressive woman. Endlessly smoking cigarettes, swearing freely and moaning in her gruff voice, she was the picture of glamour and decadence. It all made such an impression on me, and I've not forgotten a moment of it.

The time came when Barbara needed to put her dress on, and unfortunately that meant it was out of the room for Master Foreman. 'I've got you a ticket for out front,' said Barbara. 'See you after the show.'

An usher took me to a seat at the front of the stalls and I remember vividly the feeling of hundreds of eyes on me as I was escorted past them. All the other kids seemed to be wondering who the hell the kid in the suit was, and I must say I felt a bit embarrassed and a little bit special at the same time. 'If you need anything, just ask for me,' said the usher before leaving me to myself.

The curtain flew open and the show began. It was *Cinderella*, with Barbara playing the Fairy Godmother alongside Ed Stewart as Buttons, and it was fabulous. Sure, my tastes extended further than panto at that point, but as the kids screamed and the 'oh no you don'ts' echoed around the theatre I was totally seduced by it all. I shouted my heart out until the curtain finally fell, and before I knew it I was being led backstage again.

'Well, what did you think?' asked Barbara, looking radiant after the show.

'Absolutely fantastic,' I enthused.

'That's wonderful, darling,' she said. 'Now, tell me what it is you want to do.'

If I'd been a little unsure of my reasons for wanting to act when I'd spoken to Dad, there wasn't a doubt in my mind now. My visit to the theatre had blown me away. I had the bug already. I knew it.

'I want to be an actor,' I said with a big smile. 'And I want to go to stage school.'

Barbara nodded. 'Well, there's a few to choose from. There's Corona and Barbara Speake, both great schools, but I think you couldn't do much better than Italia Conti. It's one of the best, so I say give them a try.'

Sage advice. Without it I wouldn't have had a clue where to start. Barbara explained how I should apply. I needed to send off for a prospectus, and prepare for an audition, which involved memorising a few monologues. Nerve-racking stuff for a kid who'd only been in a few school plays, but so exciting and dreamy too.

'You'll need an acting coach to get you ready for the audition,' added Barbara. 'I'll try and find someone for you who's round your way and you can take it from there.'

In such a short space of time, it felt like Barbara had done so much to set me on the right path. I couldn't thank her enough.

'Don't even think about it, darling, it's a pleasure,' she told me. 'Anything for Freddie's son. But listen to me when I say this. Nobody will ever help you in this business. The only person who can really help you is yourself. If you want it bad enough, you've got to go out and get it. There's no substitute for hard work, self-belief, energy and dedication, and once you leave here today you're on your own when it comes to finding work.'

I listened intently. Barbara was deadly serious, and it was in those moments that I began to appreciate what a challenge becoming a successful actor would be. It didn't put me off, though, but only strengthened my resolve to get out there and get stuck in.

When Barbara said she'd get me a cab to take me home, my heart began to sink. Everything had been so wonderful. I'd been catapulted into a strange, thrilling new world and it had all gone so quickly. I didn't want it to end so soon.

'Oh, I thought there was another show today,' I said, hoping she would take the hint.

'You want to see it *again*?' said Barbara with a smile.

'Well, if that's all right with...'

''Course it is!' She sounded delighted, and laughed a little as she turned to Annie Ross. 'Here, Annie, he wants to stay for the next show.'

'Oh no,' joked Annie, a cigarette poised in her hand. 'He's hooked. Another one who's been bitten by the bug.'

Barbara nodded and looked at me with a glint in her eye. 'You'll do,' she said. 'You'll do.'

During the break between the matinee and the evening performance, Barbara wanted to do a bit of shopping, so we headed off down the high street. Barbara is a British icon, and I'll never forget how she handled all the people who wanted to speak to her or ask her for an autograph. She was so gracious. She had a smile and a word for everyone, and I could tell from their faces how much it meant to them. I could imagine them telling their friends about it. 'You'll never guess who I met today – Barbara Windsor! And she was lovely!' The public think of Barbara as one of their own and she never disappoints. I learned a great lesson in humility that afternoon, and I'll never forget what she did for me. The memory always makes me feel emotional, and, looking back, I realise what a turning point it was in my life. Barbara, thank you. You are a star!

I saw the show again, then a cab whisked me back to Dulwich and Mum. 'So, how'd it go?' she asked excitedly.

'Well...' I began, and off I went with my story. What a whirlwind the day had been. By the time I stopped speaking, Mum was as high as I was.

The next day Ronnie Knight called up with a message from Barbara. Ronnie said how she had really enjoyed having me over, and that Mum and Dad should be proud of the way I conducted myself. Such kind words. It meant a lot to see Mum's face light up in a way I hadn't seen for a long time.

Dad had started the ball rolling, and now it was up to me and Mum to keep it going. Thanks to Barbara, we knew what to do next. We applied to Italia Conti and received a prospectus and application form for an audition. Mum and I sat down together and began to fill it in. On the form there was a box asking for my religion, so I put in 'Church of England'.

'You can't put that!' said Mum when she saw what I'd written.

'What?' I said. 'But we are Church of England.'

'Rub it out,' she replied.

I didn't have a clue what was going on, and told her I couldn't rub it out. The marks would look terrible.

'Then add "becoming R.C.",' she insisted.

'What are you talking about?'

'*Italia* Conti,' she said pointedly. 'Italians are all Roman Catholics, aren't they, so put "becoming R.C.".'

After a futile debate I grudgingly added the words. I thought it was a bit crazy, but, hey, what did I know? Mums are always right, eh!

That done, it was time to make sure I had something to perform when I turned up at the audition. On Barbara's recommendation I went to see Mrs Price, an acting and elocution coach who had a small studio in Streatham. She was a demure, gently spoken lady with a wonderfully tolerant, patient demeanour. Just as well because I was as green as green could be.

Mrs Price quickly gauged my strengths and chose material she felt would best suit me. I needed two pieces – one from Shakespeare and another piece of prose – so she selected a Puck speech from *A Midsummer Night's*

Dream and a monologue by the Artful Dodger from Dickens's *Oliver Twist*. Can you see a pattern emerging? Ironically, the Dodger speech was the one describing seeing Bill Sykes meeting his gruesome end, a scene I was to enact many years later when I played Bill in a film version of the book. Anyway, I digress.

The song we chose was 'Morning Has Broken', which had recently been a hit for Cat Stevens, one of my favourite singers. Unfortunately, we discovered that the only thing broken was my voice. I couldn't sing a note. We tried some other tunes without much success and eventually decided to stick with what we had.

I had to prepare a dance too, but that is a memory I have well and truly erased any trace of. What I do know is that Mrs Price worked hard under the premise that I wanted to be an actor, not a song and dance man. She did her best to help me, while I diligently learned my lines and practised every day with the help of my mum and my sister.

Audition day finally came around. I had never been so nervous in my life. As Mum and I sat waiting in the main reception area at Italia Conti, I couldn't believe my eyes. Boarding school it certainly was not. We were surrounded by pictures of former pupils such as Gertrude Lawrence and Noel Coward, piano music filled the air and the sound of classes of children singing scales and dance teachers barking routines echoed around the corridors. And then there were the girls. Oh boy! I'd never seen so many lovely young ladies in one place.

They kept running past in leotards, giggling and flirting; their hair up in ponytails, their faces all made up. The school's uniform policy seemed to insist that they wore short skirts and the place had a lot of big staircases. Need I say more? If that wasn't an incentive to do my best, I didn't know what was. A Churchill speech could not have been more inspiring than the sight of so many pretty girls. 'Focus, Jamie!' I kept saying to myself. 'Focus!'

Italia Conti had sent a list of what I should wear – T-shirt, dance shoes and knitted trousers. Mum and I had absolutely no idea what knitted trousers were. I turned up in a suit with a pair of tennis shoes under my arm. I'll never forget being in the changing room with the other auditionees all dressed in the right gear and sneering at me in my shirt and tie. I'll show you, I thought. Eventually, my name was called. Mum handed me my sheet music. 'Jamie, if you don't get this audition I'm going to punch you all the way up the fucking street,' she said. She sounded pretty serious too.

My nerves were really getting the better of me as I walked into the little audition room. What a sight I must have been for the two ladies who were there to greet me. There was Miss Brearley and old Miss Conti, the last surviving member of the Conti family – two doyennes of the theatre world who had seen it all and worked with the best. They smiled encouragingly and asked me to give my music to the pianist. There was an air of calm and quiet in the room that only made me more nervous as I walked back from the piano and stood waiting in the middle of the room.

'What have you got for us today?' asked Miss Conti. 'Tell us what you'd like to begin with.'

'I'll do me song first,' I said, as upbeat as I could. Get the painful bit over first, Jamie, I thought.

'And what will that be?' they enquired.

'"Morning Has Broken".'

This was received with arched eyebrows. They obviously knew something I didn't. Oh dear, I thought, as the piano struck up the tune that had become the bane of my life over the past few weeks. I began to warble my way through the opening lines and, by the time I got to the second verse, I already felt like the morning *was* broken. It was a disaster, and I knew it. My heart sank further with every syllable of the bloody song.

'Stop, stop, stop!' I said to the pianist, who seemed more than happy to oblige. The room went quiet. The ladies looked at me wide-eyed.

'I'm sorry, I'm not a very good singer,' I explained, stating the bleeding obvious.

They smiled condescendingly and waited for me to continue.

'How about I do me Puck for you?' I said, trying to keep things moving.

They patiently waited for me to continue. I remembered Mrs Price's advice: breathe deep, try to relax. Easy for her to say. I settled myself as best I could and began.

When it was over I felt it had gone well and my confidence began to return ever so slightly. At least the ladies no longer had that horrified look on their faces. It was time for my next act.

'What have you chosen for your prose?' they asked.

'The Artful Dodger from Charles Dickens's *Oliver Twist*.'

The ladies nodded politely, but didn't look too impressed. From the way I looked and spoke, they were probably thinking I *was* the Artful Dodger. Still, I gave it my all. Then I moved on to what must have been the most ridiculous little dance routine they had ever seen. Both of them looked quite relieved when it was over.

'That's fine. Please wait outside, Jamie,' said Miss Brearley, giving nothing away.

I collected my sheet music from the pianist, who winked at me sympathetically. I smiled weakly but was totally dejected.

Oh God! I thought, as I left the room. What had I been thinking? I'm no actor, I was saying to myself, and I'm certainly not Fred Astaire. Why didn't I pick something by Frank Sinatra? I grew up with Frank's music, so at least I might have finished the fucking song. I thought of Mrs Price again, who'd drummed into me,

'Whatever happens, just keep going.' So much for that pearl of wisdom.

After an interminable wait in the corridor, they finally called me back in.

'I don't think that went too well, did it?' I asked.

'Why do you want to come to this school?' came Miss Brearley's reply.

'Because I want to be an actor,' I said.

'Can you tell us *why*?'

Whatever I said, I must have said it with passion. I do remember I told them about my love of film, my theatre experiences and the actors I admired. I told them how determined I was to learn a craft that I had so much admiration and respect for, and that I was ready to give it my total dedication. If my audition performances hadn't been what they were looking for, then I must have said something to impress them. For what came next was a total shock.

'We've made a decision,' began Miss Brearley.

Here it comes, I thought. Shoulders back, Jamie. Chin up. Take it like a man.

'But first we must tell you something. That was the worst audition we've seen in 30 years...'

That's a bit strong, I thought. Me Puck had gone well, hadn't it?

'...The last person who auditioned that badly was Anthony Newley,' she continued. 'You're in.'

At first I didn't register past the 'worst audition' bit.

Bollocks! I thought. What am I going to do now? For a couple of seconds I was truly gutted. But suddenly it hit me they'd said something else. What was that about Anthony Newley? Had I heard them say I was in?

'Did you say I'm in?' I said, looking up incredulously. '*In?*'

'Yes, Jamie. We've accepted you. Congratulations. But you are going to have to work very hard. Don't let us down.'

'Thank you so much,' I said, dumbfounded. At least my mum wasn't going to punch me up the street. I could barely take it in. One second I thought it was curtains for my acting career, the next thing I knew I was being told I had a place at the famous Italia Conti Stage School. I left the room dazed, happy and a little confused.

Mum was waiting for me outside, all smiles and excitement. 'How did you get on?' she asked.

'I think I'm in,' I told her.

She gave me a big hug, but warned me not to get too excited. After all, not everyone had auditioned, and nothing was official yet. I'd been told I was accepted, but only on the quiet. There was nothing to do but stay calm and wait for the other kids to finish.

Eventually I was called into the main office, and introduced to Mrs Sheward, a prim and stern-looking lady wearing a frilly blouse, pearls and a cardigan over her shoulders. Her hair was swept up into a bun and her glasses were perched near the end of her nose. At first her school-ma'am look frightened the life out of me, but what she had to say soon put me at ease.

'I don't know what you did, Jamie, but they've taken a shine to you,' said Mrs Sheward with a smile. 'They think you have something to offer, so I'm pleased to welcome you to Italia Conti.'

This was it. This was the moment I'd been hoping for, and now it had arrived it was like I was floating on air. I felt I'd come so far, a feeling that was heightened when Mrs Sheward told me how many kids hadn't been accepted. I was one of only a handful picked for that year. I felt so proud.

My face said it all when I walked out to meet Mum, and she was totally made up. 'You did it, Jamie!' she said as she hugged me. 'And you were wearing a suit.'

She was right. We laughed together and as I stood there I noticed a picture up on the wall. It was Anthony Newley smiling down on me. I laughed a little bit. How did I get away with that? I thought. At the same time I told myself I'd have my picture up on that wall one day, whatever it took. And I'm happy to say I now do.

I'd walked into that audition as a boy in the doldrums. A boy who hadn't been to school in ages. A boy whose life was going nowhere fast. A boy whose father was in prison. Being accepted, getting a place in that most prestigious academy, made me realise how lost I'd been. Suddenly having a future, a new direction, made me feel good in a way I hadn't for a long, long time.

What with Dad being away, we were pretty hard up at the time, but Mum had set aside some money to take me out for a little celebration. Off we went for a glass of wine and a meal, and it was one of the happiest moments of those bleak years when my dear father was away from us. Mum raised a toast to me, and to our family. 'You wait till we tell your dad,' she said. 'He'll be so proud.'

We told Dad on our next visit to the Scrubs, and he was delighted. Buster and Jimmy were in the visiting room, and all of them looked so pleased as they toasted me.

Later that year I received a present that, considering how little money was knocking about, came as a huge surprise: a beautiful long stereo system with a smoked plastic top. It was a state-of-the-art Bush with a record deck on one side, a radio and four-track tape deck on the other. I'd wanted one for ages, but not for a second had I expected to get my hands on such a top-notch piece of kit. I'll never forget unwrapping it and staring up at Mum, mouth agape.

'That's from your dad to say how proud he is you got into Conti's,' she said.

She didn't need to say any more. I could feel the tears welling in my eyes. It was the best Christmas present I ever had.

Things were looking up, and I had a new vocation. It was time to go to work.

7

THE WORLD'S A STAGE

What have I let myself in for? I thought. I was staring at a timetable Italia Conti had posted to me to give me a flavour of what I'd be getting up to at stage school. There were acting classes, sure, but on top of them were ballet lessons, tap lessons, singing lessons and, worse, maths, reading and writing lessons. An awful load of lessons I wasn't interested in, in other words. I was only interested in the boxes that had 'acting' in them somewhere. Still, I supposed I was willing to give all the other stuff a shot. The main thing was I was off to become an actor, and I felt like the luckiest kid in the world.

These days the Italia Conti School is at the Barbican,

north of the river, but back then it was in Landor Road down in Clapham North, on the site of the old Avondale Dance Hall. My dad had spent a lot of time there in the fifties, no doubt doing a bit of business and having a good time with his mates. It was nice to feel a link to Dad's past, but the only parallel would have been the girls. Put simply, whatever Dad had been up to down the Avondale, he wasn't carrying a pair of ballet shoes in his bag.

My first day was weird, to put it mildly. For a start, I'd been at an all boys' school since my primary, and it was a big shock to the system to be suddenly surrounded by hundreds of pretty girls strutting around in miniskirts. A very welcome shock, mind you. Being performers, they weren't shy, and it was quite something to come up against such extrovert and flirtatious young women. I was like a fox in a chicken pen. All those lovely, long legs and fluttering eyelashes certainly gave me pause for thought – and, after a moment of deliberation, I quickly concluded I was in heaven!

Another shock was the theatricality of everyone and everything at the school. I'd been used to boys' stuff – football, rugby, cricket – and boys' games, and this new, alien environment took a bit of adjusting to. But, being me, it didn't take long to assert myself and start flirting with the girls and making the boys laugh. As for the maths, reading and writing classes, I soon realised they weren't for me.

Although I've always been an avid reader, academia wasn't my bag at that age. I just wanted to do as much acting as possible, so I decided to go my own way. Whenever I had any 'academic' classes, I'd bunk off and sneak into a senior acting class or two. I built up a strong rapport with the teachers and, seeing how keen I was, they ended up giving me carte blanche when it came to diving in and out of classes.

I'd been given a great chance to shine and I was determined to grasp it with both hands. In those first few months, I was like a sponge, soaking up everything around me, and the acting classes were a revelation. I was introduced to a world of techniques by teachers who pushed you hard to bring the best out in you. I loved improvisation, which gave me enormous freedom to express myself; a freedom that, having come from the regimented confines of boarding school, I'd only ever experienced on the sports field. I quickly realised that, far from being out of my depth, I had found my spiritual home, and soon recognised it was a matter of confidence and self-belief – two things I'd never been short of.

I settled in almost immediately and I think everyone took to me straight away, especially Mrs Sheward and her lovely daughter Anne, who ran the school's agency. Thanks to her, within just a few months I was rewarded with my first professional audition. And what an audition it was: an opportunity to join the greatest theatre company in the world – the National Theatre at the Old Vic – at that time under the artistic directorship of the greatest actor in the world, Sir Laurence Olivier.

It might sound strange, but I wasn't nervous. I'd been nervous auditioning for a place at the school, but now I was there it all felt like the most natural thing in the world. Obviously the harsher realities of life at home allowed me to put things into perspective. When your dad's away in prison, it's his welfare that keeps you awake at night, not getting a part in some play. Also, I felt older than my years and was very comfortable around adults. I'd been around them all my life in the pub, after all. Perversely, I think it was my relaxed attitude to the acting world that gave me an edge at my first audition.

I was with Stephen Benton and Steven Howell – a couple of mates from school – and we set off in the company of my favourite chaperone, Mrs Da Costa. She was a wonderful Jewish lady with a great sense of humour that helped us to stay really relaxed. A lovely old girl.

In those days, the National had its rehearsal rooms in Aquinas Street, just off Stamford Street, in Waterloo. They were nothing fancy, just a couple of mobile homes. One was an administration block with a small canteen, the other the main rehearsal room. We were in the canteen, waiting for rehearsals to break for lunch, when all of a sudden the doors flew open and in flew some 'luvvies'. But these weren't just any luvvies; these were

Larry Olivier's luvvies, the crème de la crème of British theatre actors: Dennis Quilley, Sir Michael Hordern, Anna Carteret, Clive Merrison, John Shrapnel – the list could go on and on.

I felt my pulse quicken as they filled the room with such exuberance and laughter. I felt that buzz again, the same buzz I'd had in Barbara's dressing room. I wanted to be a part of this, I was *going* to be a part of this. This was where I wanted to be.

The audition was for *The Front Page*, the comedy classic by Ben Hecht and Charles MacArthur, and I was up for the role of 'Boy Scout', a 'walk-on' part. The great Michael Blakemore was directing. I was called into a room and soon found myself being scrutinised by Michael and his assistant. Michael looked me up and down, did a bit of chin-stroking, then gave his verdict on the little boy standing there doing his best 'Boy Scout' impression.

'No, I don't see him as Macduff's son...' he began.

Macduff. *Macduff*. Who the hell's Macduff? I thought. There'd been some mistake. I wasn't there to be anyone's son; I wanted to be the one in the neckerchief and woggle! I wasn't happy and, not being versed in the dos and don'ts of being 15 and dealing with a great director, felt like I should say something. I've never been backward about coming forward, even then.

'...no, no, no, definitely not Macduff's son,' continued Michael.

I was just on the brink of putting Mr Blakemore straight when the young male assistant shook his head at me and winked, as if to say, 'Don't worry.' He leaned into Michael and whispered that they were also looking for 'Boy Scout' replacements in *The Front Page*.

'Ah yes, yes,' exclaimed Michael. 'Now, I *do* see him as a Boy Scout.'

Phew, I thought, we're finally on track. Not getting a part is one thing, but not getting a part you didn't even go for… well, that's just not cricket!

'You'll do,' declared Michael grandly.

I smiled and nodded 'thanks' to the assistant.

I'd got it. My first audition and I'd got the part. I tried not to look too excited as I glided out of the room, yet I could have punched the sky. There was no time for any of that, though, for on my way back to the canteen I noticed a very tall, powerfully built man coming down the corridor towards me. It took me a couple of seconds to realise who it was.

It was Laurence Olivier. *Now* I was nervous.

As we got closer I felt my palms getting sweaty. Olivier, I was thinking, it's Olivier. What should I say? What should I call him? What am I doing? It was best not to say anything. Just keep my mouth shut and smile. I kept moving, but as we were about to pass each other he stopped and blocked me off. I looked up at him and gave my best polite smile. Sir Laurence looked down at me imperiously for a few seconds. My heart was thumping in my chest so much I was sure he could hear it. Then suddenly he broke into a wonderful, broad smile.

'So how did it go?' he enquired.

'It went really well, thank you very much. I got the part.'

'Oh, well done,' he said. 'Congratulations and welcome to the company.'

What a man. What a moment. If that wasn't a sign, an omen, that I had a future in this profession, I don't know what is. I scuttled past him and rejoined the others in the canteen.

Mrs Da Costa asked me how I'd got on, but I'd forgotten about my good news.

'I just spoke to Laurence Olivier,' I said.

'That's nice, darling,' she said, as if I'd told her I like baked beans on toast.

'What about the audition?'

'Oh, oh, I got it,' I stuttered.

'That's nice, darling,' she repeated. 'I knew you would.'

I was so made up about getting the part, but was on a bigger high from my encounter in the corridor. I rushed to the nearest phone box to tell Mum, and she was delighted. Again she said how proud Dad would be, and again I couldn't wait to tell him. Mum also told me what an honour it was to have the chance to work at the National, and added that we knew quite a few of the stage hands because her family was from the area.

It was lovely to know that they would keep an eye out for me.

The Front Page turned out to be a huge success, and being part of it was a thrill from start to finish. My bit came at a very tense point in the play when hard-boiled Chicago newspaper editor Walter Burns sends his crony Diamond Louie to find some muscle to help him move a desk which contains a condemned man in hiding. The crony gets it all wrong and comes back with three boy scouts and a tramp. Cue me and two other scouts running on to the stage, saluting Walter Burns and promptly being booted off with a 'Get them out of here!' Off we'd run, all the way back to our dressing room at the top of the Old Vic, and it was always a fabulous feeling to hear the audience still laughing when we got there.

On the first night I was racked with nerves and couldn't bring myself to look at the audience as I gave my first professional performance. Mum was there, of course, as she would be for so many future productions. It goes without saying that I so wished Dad was there for my debut, but as a family we all just had to accept the way things were and take it in our stride. I kept telling myself that one day there would come a time...

I received £1.38 a performance, a bit of a pittance really, but I wasn't doing it for the money. Mum was so proud of me that she wouldn't let me cash my pay

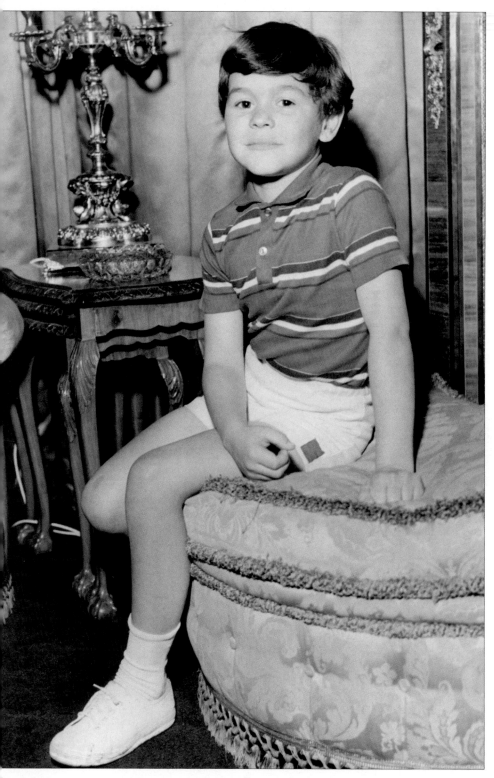

Brought up to be a straight-goer – this photo was taken when I was ten years old, just before Dad went to prison for his involvement with the murder of Jack 'The Hat' McVitie.

Above: The Foreman kids: me, my sister Danielle and my older brother, Gregory.

Below left: Angelic, moi?

Below right: My mum and dad in the sixties with Dad's great friend Ronnie Oliffe.

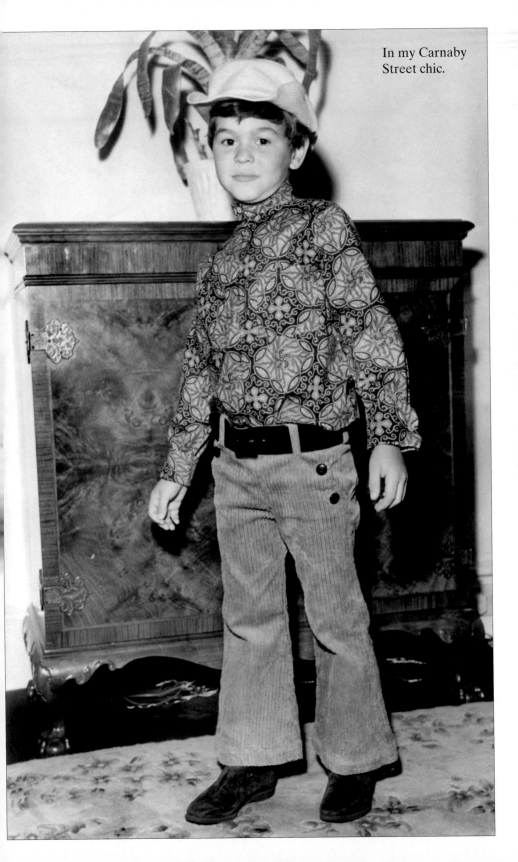

In my Carnaby
Street chic.

Holding On was my first decent break in television – and my first bed scene!

With friend and co-star Richard Willis in *A Bunch of Fives*. The director, John Sichel, pushed me hard to get the best out of me and I learned a lot from him.

Our Show was a Saturday morning programme which went out straight after *Tiswas*. My job was to interview heroes of the day such as Carrie Fisher and Terry Venables – and I had an absolute ball! The bottom photo shows me with some of the other presenters: Elvis Payne, Graham Fletcher, Melissa Wilkes and Susan Tully (who went on to star as Michelle in *EastEnders*).

© *Rex Features*

Above: With my great mates John Bunce (left) and Pandy (right).

Below: The George Washington Motel in Allentown, Pennsylvania, where I played the waiting game on the journey to meet my father in America.

Customs man shot dead in £1m drug hunt

By T. A. SANDROCK, Crime Correspondent

A CUSTOMS investigator was shot dead in Commercial Road, Stepney, yesterday as a joint Customs-police team to which he belonged neared a culmination in an 18-month drug-smuggling inquiry.

The investigator, Mr Peter Bennett, 32, a married man, with a year-old son, was killed after Customs officials followed a lorry through the East End.

Last night a man was being questioned at Limehouse police station.

A Customs Official said later that 19 people were detained and cannabis resin worth at least £1 million found during Customs and police activity yesterday. Later, four more people were held.

Mr Bennett, who lived in Twickenham, was shot after the lorry which had been followed stopped in Commercial Road near Lowell Street.

A man got out of the cab and was approached by Customs officers. He fired a shot from a small automatic pistol, hitting Mr Bennett.

As shoppers and children ran for cover the man was away chased by other members of the Customs and police team. He lost one of his shoes during the chase.

Man wounded

As two officers closed on him, he fired again, possibly with the intention of shooting himself, and fell wounded to the pavement.

Mr Lawrence Lane, 25, a warehouseman, said: "Two men came up to a man who was being chased and grappled with him, shouting to an elderly man with a walking stick who was standing nearby: 'Hit him, hit him.'"

Mrs Gloria Ebsworth, who works in a snack bar opposite the scene of the shooting, said she heard a woman standing at a bus stop scream. When she looked round she saw a man fall in the roadway.

"Then I saw someone helping him and other men ran after a fellow, grab him and they were sitting on top of him."

Mr Bennett is believed to be the first Customs officer to be

Continued on Back P. Col 5

PHOTO OF 'DUKE' ISSUED

By T. A. SANDROCK Crime Correspondent

A PHOTOGRAPH of Colin Osbourne, 50, known as "The Duke," was issued yesterday by Hampshire police who are trying to trace him in connection with a £2 million cannabis smuggling investigation.

Until recently, Osbourne had been living at Wallington, Surrey. He is 6ft 1in tall and nobby.

ally wears a wig because of an illness which causes hair to fall out.

A man was charged yesterday with the murder of a Customs officer, Mr Peter Bennett, 32, who was shot dead when the container lorry in which the cannabis was hidden was seized in East London last Friday.

Leonard Edward Charles Watkins, 40, a garage proprietor whose address is unknown, will appear at Thames court today.

Seven people are to appear in court at Portsmouth today charged with Customs offences after the drugs haul, in East London

British Customs officials and Hampshire detectives were in Holland last night interviewing two men detained by Dutch police.

Drug swoop squad hunt for The Duke

By ALAN GORDON and BARRY WIGMORE

ARMED police were last night hunting a man nicknamed The Duke.

They want to question him about a huge drug-smuggling racket involving millions of pounds.

Detectives warned that the man may be armed and that the public should not try to tackle him.

"He must not be approached," they said.

The alert went out after Customs men and police cut open a container lorry suspected of being used to smuggle drugs into Britain.

Hidden in a secret compartment was a ton and a quarter of "Pakistani Black" cannabis resin worth more than £2 million in street sales.

Seized

The lorry was seized on Friday in the East End of London. Customs investigator Peter Bennett was shot dead when the

drugs team swooped.

The man known as The Duke is 50-year-old Colin Osbourne, whose address was a flat in an expensive block at Beddington Gardens, Wallington, Surrey.

Police said that Osbourne, who is 6 ft. 1 in. tall, suffers from a scalp complaint that causes his hair to fall out in tufts.

When last seen, he was wearing a reddish brown Afro-style wig.

A neighbour at the Wallington flat said last night: "Mr Osbourne was very polite. He said he was in the music business."

OSBOURNE: Hunted by drugs team

FIND THE DUKE!

THIS is the man known as The Duke, who was being hunted last night in connection with a multi-million-pound drugs racket.

He is 50-year-old Colin Osbourne, owner of a £50,000 penthouse in Wallington, Surrey.

Police warned: "Do not approach him. He may well be armed."

Osbourne, who is 6ft. 1in. tall, wears a wig to cover baldness. He dresses in trendy clothes and enjoys the company of young men.

Police staged several raids in London last night looking for him. They said he was "of prime importance" in a major drugs investigation code-named Operation Wrecker.

Thirty-seven people have already been questioned about huge shipments of cannabis from Pakistan to Britain. Seven have been charged with offences connected with importing and supplying cannabis.

Customs undercover man Peter Bennett, 32, was shot dead on Friday when he approached a suspect lorry in London's East End.

How the newspapers reported the shooting of the customs officer and the hunt for 'Dukey' Osbourne.

Top left and right
© The Daily Telegraph

Middle and bottom © Mirrorpix

cheques. 'I'll give you the money, Jamie,' I remember her saying, 'but I'm going to put these in a scrapbook.'

It meant so much to Mum that I was making something of myself, and this meant the world to me. I wanted to do something to thank her for everything and make her feel as special as she made me feel.

One night I got free tickets for the opening of Franco Zeffirelli's production of *Saturday, Sunday, Monday* and decided to take Mum. When we got to the theatre I realised it was the first time I'd be using the front entrance – up till then I'd only ever slipped in and out of the stage door. Just as we were about to go in, Mum stopped suddenly. A strange, wistful look came over her face. She turned and looked out across Baylis Road.

'You know what?' she said, taking my hand. 'When I was a little girl we used to stand over the road as the carriages pulled up on first nights. We'd watch all the rich and famous of the day getting out with their top hats and their furs and diamonds. It seemed like another world. Now here I am standing here with my son.'

Mum was brought up in Baylis Road – or Oakley Street as it was in her day – and the look on her face said it all. She'd also come a long way, my mum. I looked at her for a few moments and smiled. 'Come on,' I said, giving her a little squeeze, 'take my arm and let me buy you a drink.' We waltzed in together arm in arm.

The atmosphere inside was magic. You really can't beat the feeling of electricity and anticipation in the air on a first night. We went to the bar and – using the money I'd saved up from my Boy Scout part – I bought us a bottle of champagne. Looking around, I recognised so many faces in the room, and I suddenly felt so at home as Mum and I touched glasses. Other actors and members of the company came up to say hello, and I introduced them to Mum. I had a wonderful feeling of acceptance within the acting community, and it all felt so natural. It wasn't that I thought I'd arrived. Far from it. The day an actor thinks like that is the day they sign their own death warrant. But I did think I might be on my way, that I might have a place in this business.

The performance was fantastic, with a sterling cast that included Laurence Olivier, Frank Finlay and Joan Plowright. It doesn't get much better than that. The play is about the breakdown of a family, and most of the action takes place in an Italian kitchen. The funny thing was that every scene involved food – Zeffirelli had brought in an Italian chef to prepare it offstage. The mother, played by Joan, kept serving up loads of lovely Italian dishes to her family. They were constantly eating, and all these fantastic smells were wafting around the auditorium. By the time the curtain fell, we were as interested in the pasta as we were in the play – and absolutely starving. Mum and I walked out of the theatre and across the road into an Italian trattoria in the Cut. That night is such a warm, wonderful memory.

I must have done something right at the National, for

when *The Front Page* came to an end they asked me to stay on and do another 'walk on' in Chekhov's masterpiece *The Cherry Orchard*. The great actress Constance Cummings was starring, and I was to play a peasant 'stable boy'. At the beginning of the play, when the family arrived at their country estate, a little girl and boy (played by yours truly) ran forward and presented Miss Cummings with a bunch of flowers. The girl tore my serf's cap from my disrespectful head and hit me with it. She curtsied, I bowed, and we ran off. A lovely little part, that always got a laugh!

Maybe I was born a chameleon, or maybe the circumstances of my upbringing turned me into one – who knows? – but I was drinking in every minute of my life. I'd made new friends and opened my mind up to a whole new way of being. But I was carrying a secret with me. For quite a while nobody at Conti's knew who I was or what world I came from. As far as the school was concerned, my dad was 'away on business'. There was simply no need for anyone to know different, and I was comfortable being between two worlds again.

Then, one day, the two worlds collided.

There was a secondary school near to Conti's, and some of the kids there were a right bunch of hooligans. They didn't like us and we didn't think much of them either. Quite predictable really, when you consider how different the two schools were. We stayed out of one another's way most of the time, and that was that. Until, that is, things began to get a bit nasty.

I was with my best mate Pandy – short for Pandalis – one afternoon. Pandy was the first bloke I'd spoken to at Conti's. He was in the class above me and approached me one day with, 'So you're the new boy, are you?'

'That's right,' I replied.

There was a bit of friction, and we could have taken an instant dislike to each other, but thankfully the complete opposite happened. We obviously liked each other's no-nonsense attitude, for, in that briefest of encounters, we clicked out of mutual respect. We quickly discovered we were kindred spirits and became best mates. Thick as thieves. I am privileged to say that our friendship remains solid and strong to this day. Pandy is a great friend and a stand-up guy. He has stood by me through thick and thin and helped me immeasurably when things have been tough. I trust him with anything, and he is even godfather to my son Alfie.

Pandy was the only person at the school who knew about Dad. We had that between us, plus he was a good fighter and knew how to look after himself, unlike *some* of the other boys at the school, bless 'em.

Anyway, school was over, and Pandy and me were walking up Landor Road towards the café we always frequented before the pubs opened, when suddenly we were met with a horrible scene. A gang of hooligans were giving some of the girls from Conti's a load of grief. We'd seen it all before – local girls standing there with their boyfriends and mouthing off. Our girls – who were a damn sight prettier and classier than the locals – used to just brush it off and move on. Still, it wasn't nice. We felt very protective towards our girls, and as time wore on the situation had begun to give me and Pandy the right hump.

On this occasion, as we eyed the usual suspects hurling their filthy abuse, we decided that enough was enough. We kicked off. Pandy steamed in with a couple of right-handers, and I chinned a few of them and sent them running. It was all over for the afternoon, and we were glad we'd made a stand, but we knew full well that it wouldn't be the end of it. The question was, would me and Pandy be able to handle things if more of them came back? It turned out to be a question we didn't need to answer.

The very next afternoon there was a squad car stationed outside the school – Conti's had got wind of what had gone down and called the police. But the police weren't the only ones there to guard us against trouble. There was also a group of solid-looking men, and I knew every single one of them.

When I'd told Mum what had happened, she'd been as appalled as I was about what was going on outside my school every day. 'I wish you'd said something earlier, Jamie,' she'd said, picking up the phone. Mum had put in a call to Ronnie Oliffe, and the next thing I knew Ron had assembled a crew of chaps – his brother Danny, my mum's brother, Freddie Puttnan (a beautiful man, God rest his soul), my cousin Barbie's husband, Dave, and some other friends of the family – to escort us all out of school the next day.

The police must have wondered what the hell was going on. There they were in their uniforms outside a prestigious stage school, and alongside them were a handful of faces they recognised from South London's underworld.

'Who are all these men?' said one of the officers to our headmaster, Don Sheward.

His response was priceless: 'Concerned parents.' The head must have cottoned on that these men were in some way linked to me and my father, but his lips were sealed. Good old Don – I think he got a bit of a buzz from it!

'Oh,' said the policeman, 'you don't need us then.' The copper would have known full well that, if my dad's men were involved in this, Italia Conti had nothing to worry about. The police drove off and left us to it.

For the first time in a long time, all the Conti girls filed out of the gates with not so much as a peep from any locals. I'd managed to get hold of the names of some of the troublemakers, and afterwards my uncle Fred went knocking on a few doors. He had words with some of their dads, and the mention of my father's name meant word soon got out that there'd be trouble if anyone looked twice at the Conti girls.

We never had any grief after that, and I assume the school was grateful for what had happened. Sure, my 'secret' was out, and everyone realised there was a little more to me than they'd thought, but it didn't change a thing. My dad's name had sorted out a problem, but that didn't mean I starting carrying on like some Flash Harry. I never boasted about who Dad was – he had a good name and there was no way I was going to abuse that. I'd always fought my own battles, and only ever called for help when I really needed it. All I can say is I'm glad our family name was able to sort out the situation.

At the end of my second year at Conti's, Ronnie Oliffe set me up with a summer job in a spieler – an illegal gambling club. Ron loves a game of cards, and was only too happy to help me earn a bit of extra cash. I was young and as hungry as ever to experience London's rich tapestry. This job certainly satisfied my appetite for adventure – it was incredible.

Set up in the basement of a little hotel in Earl's Court, the club was run by a nefarious bloke who I'll call Aussie B and his crew – I won't use his real name here. Aussie B was a mad Antipodean and a right player who drove a bright-red V12 E-type Jag with whitewall tyres. What a character.

My job was to do the 'chalking up'. B had tapped into the Tannoy systems of the legitimate betting shops and, as the odds were called out for every race meeting that day, I chalked them up on to a list of the runners pinned on the wall. I had to stay sharp, as the prices were always changing and I'd get a right bollocking if I was sticking up the wrong odds. There was so much money changing hands in there, and calling a 9–1 when it was an 8–1 could make a difference of thousands of pounds. I made a few mistakes to begin with, but soon became very adept at keeping tabs on whatever the Tannoy fired out. The less scrupulous punters would try to put me off, and then argue that the odds on their nag were longer than I had chalked up. I soon cottoned on to this, though.

A lovely man called Tubba Hayes ran the book. Tubba was a good old South London fellow who'd kindly watch my back and double-check that I had the odds right. I had a lot of affection for old Tubba, even though his hygiene left a little to be desired. A big man, he always wore an open shirt and a string vest, and I don't think I ever saw him without a fag hanging out of his mouth. He created quite a stink, did Tubba, but he really looked after me down in the basement that hot summer.

The characters I met in that place. Wow! Some of our punters were men who'd do anything for a pound note. Especially the Aussies, they were all at it – good, old-fashioned thieves. When they weren't gambling, they would be out doing the jewellery cases in the West End shops. They didn't use violence, mind you: they simply went in three- or four-handed, and one would nick a tray out of a display case while the others distracted the shop

THE WORLD'S A STAGE

assistant. I'll never forget the way they used to sit around the spieler fiddling with little locks to see how quickly they could pick them, all in practice for their trips into the West End.

I didn't like some of the Aussies who used to hang about, but I remember fondly one guy who I only ever knew as 'The Bushranger' or 'Bushie', a bear of a man with a freckly face that always bore a smile. He once told me that the only two countries in the world that did not have a warrant out on him were Iceland and Greenland. 'Too cold up there for us Aussies,' he quipped. He was a thief, but a compelling character who I couldn't help liking, even when I saw him plunge a kitchen knife into a man's shoulder one night. He could be a nasty piece of work to others but he was always very nice to me. The guy he plunged was an arsehole – 'A weasel not to be trusted,' Bushie told me in his thick accent. 'A man you don't want to turn your back on, Jamie.' When Bushie extracted the knife it had curved into an L shape – it had hit the man's collarbone, so luckily it hadn't done too much damage. Spielers could be dangerous places and you had to have your wits about you.

Bimbo was another old friend of my father's who used to come in. A delightful, erudite and elegant man who dressed impeccably in silk suits and open-neck shirts, spoke very well and smoked Gauloises, Bimbo was a real dandy, a Noel Coward type who used to slip me 50 quid when he knew I was going on a date. 'Buy her a bottle of champagne,' he'd say with a wink, and off I'd go. I'll never forget Blonde Pat. I loved Pat. She was married to a lawyer, whose name I never knew, and loved a gamble. She also had a penchant for drink and fine dining in London's best establishments, and now and again she'd insist I accompany her on her outings round town. We'd drive around in her sky-blue Rolls-Royce and go for drinks at Morton's in Berkeley Square. Pat loved having me with her, and it was a marvellous eye-opener for me to watch her putting on the style. She always wore the best designer clothes – all, of course, bought from the 'hoisters', or shoplifters – and was always dripping in jewels.

I remember a night out with Pat in the famous Elysee Greek restaurant. My mum, my uncle Micky and auntie Chris were with us. Mick is a very close old friend of my dad – they go way back – and Mick and Chris mean a lot to me. The Elysee is famous for its cabaret of Greek dancing and bouzouki music, which culminates in traditional plate throwing. Plates are smashed to show appreciation, but on this occasion Pat got a bit carried away and turned over a whole table. I looked on gobsmacked as waiters scurried around to repair the damage, but the owner, George, didn't bat an eyelid.

Pat leaned over to me. 'Don't worry,' she said. 'I spend a couple of grand a week in here.' How money talks. Still, Pat received a stern look and a quiet word from

Mick – men like him and Dad like to keep a low profile, so turning over tables wasn't quite their style.

Some of the other punters at the spieler really made me laugh. There was a lovely bloke called Stuttery John, who had the worst stutter in the world. One day when it was raining and the races were off, a couple of the guys, Bruce and Colin Buick, geed up someone to go against Stuttery John in a game of snap. The bloke readily agreed, obviously thinking John wouldn't stand a chance getting the word 'snap' out quick enough. John lost the first few hands on purpose with exclamations of 'Fu... fu... fu... *fuck* it!' until his opponent got nice and comfortable. But what the other bloke didn't know was, while John was terrible with 'c's and 'k's, he was fucking dynamite with 's's. They were playing for money, and John wiped the floor with him. Seeing grown men gambling on snap was a sight to behold.

That lot were always on the hustle and would gamble on anything. I even remember them betting on which of several raindrops would run down the window the fastest, and on what fly would leave the wall first – 'I'll have a pony on the right one.' That's gamblers for you. Madness.

I was working in a proper den of iniquity, but I fell in love with it. The people I encountered were like characters out of Dickens. They came from all walks of life and were always friendly to me – as long as I did my job properly. Jovial and friendly as they were, there was one thing they were serious about: money.

I earned 50 quid a day chalking up, and then there were tips on top. Most days I'd take home between £150 and £250, six days a week, which was a fortune back then. The first time I got paid I went straight to a beautiful Italian deli in Earl's Court and loaded up with as many goodies as I could carry – salamis, cheeses, smoked salmon, pate and good bottles of wine. I picked up a present or two for my sister, and then strode home proudly with it all. I laid the bags down in the kitchen in front of Mum, and when I handed her 50 quid I thought she was going to cry. 'What's the matter, Mum?' I asked.

'That's just what your father would do,' came her reply. It was a great, great feeling to finally be able to provide for the family for the first time, and I kept helping out as often as I could.

When summer was over and the new term started at Conti's, I had grown so attached to the world I was moving in – not to mention the money – that I had a real job dragging myself away from it. In the end I struck a balance between my two lives, learning my craft by day and working down the spieler by night.

What a life I was leading. I felt like a prince in the city. London was a vast and varied playground; one moment I was with the luvvies at the National Theatre, the next I was part of an exciting and seductive subterranean world where lowlifes rubbed shoulders with the rich and powerful. It was a heady mix, and by the end of that year I was drunk on the experience of it all. In or out of acting school, the world felt truly like a stage.

But, as always, there was something missing. Dad. No matter what I did, I carried a void inside me. It gnawed away, though I suppose I learned to live with it to an extent. All I could do was try to be my usual, positive self. It had been six years now, and they'd been long years. Still, we'd always held on to the hope that Dad might be eligible for early release if he behaved himself. Some chance. Deep down, we felt the authorities would never give him parole.

But, when Christmas 1974 came around, some news arrived that made us feel as if all our Christmases had come at once. It was confirmed that Dad would be coming home. Having served over six years of his sentence, losing six months of remission for some misdemeanours, he would be released in ten months. Ten months and I'd have him back. After all we had been through, after all those years, we could all do the ten months standing on our heads. This would be our last Christmas without him.

My dad was coming home.

Overjoyed? Ecstatic? There isn't one word that could do justice to the combination of relief and excitement – of pure *emotion* – we all felt as we celebrated our final Christmas without beloved Dad. Next year would be so different.

There was a big old tree, a 'Tree of Heaven', in our front garden that towered over our house. We loved that tree, and when 'Tie A Yellow Ribbon Round The Old Oak Tree' had been a hit the previous year, me, Mum and Danielle never stopped singing it. The song is about men coming home, and the words really resonated with us. Even then, we were talking about what we'd do when Dad came out, and Mum said we'd get a massive yellow ribbon and tie it around our heavenly tree. I remember looking at the tree outside the window, and thinking, Yes, Dad would love that. Now, a year later, our lovely little daydream was going to become a reality. We'd be tying the ribbon in ten months. Or so I thought.

We never got to tie that ribbon. That winter our tree crashed into the front of the house during a storm. None of us was hurt, but looking back it was like a bad omen. One month after the tree fell, I was no longer anticipating Dad's freedom. Suddenly I was facing the possibility of my father staying behind bars for life.

8

TRIAL OF A LIFETIME

The phone rang. It was Dad. 'I've been charged with the Marks thing,' he said to Mum. 'You'd better get me a brief...'

The 'Marks thing' was about Ginger Marks, an East End face who had disappeared in 1965. Little did we know, but the police had been working the Marks case while Dad was doing his ten for McVitie, and now, just as he was about to get out, they wanted to charge my father with his murder.

The way they cornered Dad was pretty low. He was in the laundry one day when a couple of screws told him he had a visit, even though it wasn't visiting day. It wasn't the first time this had happened. Not long before, Dad's father had been ill and Dad had been given a compassionate day release to see him. The screws had surprised him then, and now they were back. Dad immediately accepted the visit, worried there was some more bad news about his family. He was taken into a room and instantly recognised the two men sitting there. Two police officers, Chalk and Troon. They said they wanted to talk about Ginger.

This was no visit: it was an interrogation. Dad had been set up and he wasn't having any of it. 'I've got nothing to say to any of you,' he said. 'Now let me out of here before I smash the door down.'

The screws realised Dad wasn't mucking about, and took him back to the wing. Soon afterwards he was taken to Arbour Square Police Station in Stepney for questioning, but his only answer to whatever they came at him with was: 'No comment.' Next came the formal murder charge. Three of Dad's friends and associates were also accused of being involved: Alf Gerrard, Jerry Callaghan and Ronnie Everett.

It was a terrifying situation. Just when we were about to get Dad back, there was a chance he would be snatched away from us again. Mum must have been even more worried than me, because she knew the full extent of Dad's involvement with Ginger Marks. I didn't know the details back then, but now I'm at liberty to tell what went down between my dad's firm and Ginger.

It was a family matter that began in 1964. Ginger

Marks was a close friend of a safe-blower called Jimmy Evans – a nasty bastard obsessed with guns and violence, and a jealous maniac to boot. My dad's brother George had an affair with Pat Evans, Evans's wife. Pat was scared of her husband, and fell deeply in love with George. They used to meet secretly at a flat in Stepney, but nevertheless Evans grew highly suspicious and found out what was happening. He vowed to track down my uncle George and kill him.

After a failed attempt by Evans to shoot George at the Stepney flat – George was outside and talking to several people, so Evans bottled it – he got hold of a sawn-off shotgun and decided to do the job at George's marital home. Evans wanted an accomplice, and that's where Ginger Marks came in.

Another of their associates, David Norman, drove Evans and Marks to Uncle George's flat in Lambeth Walk. It was dark, and, having removed the lightbulb from George's landing, the two men went to work. Marks knocked on the door while Evans waited out of sight. George answered, and Marks pretended he had the wrong address before going away. They'd established my uncle was in. Now it was Evans's turn.

A second knock on the door. As it opened, Evans stepped forwards and blasted George point-blank in the groin with both barrels of the sawn-off. The impact sent him flying to the back of the hallway. George would have died if it hadn't been for a Polish neighbour who heard the blast and phoned an ambulance. It took several operations to fix him. Dear George narrowly escaped a leg amputation, and in the end was left with one testicle and a big chunk out of his leg.

Dad rushed to the hospital and was angered and devastated by what had happened. The brothers had always been so close, and seeing George lying at death's door made Dad hungry for one thing: revenge. He leaned down and whispered in George's ear. 'Give me a name,' demanded Dad.

'Ginger Marks and Jimmy Evans.'

Dad was the only person George said a word to. There was no way he was going to grass to the police, even on someone who'd tried to kill him. It's the way of the underworld. The underworld metes out its own justice, its own retribution, and it was up to Dad to make sure the job got done. It wasn't long before he received a tip-off that gave him his chance.

Evans was set to rob a jeweller's in Bethnal Green, and Marks would be with him along with three others. The date was set for 2 January 1965. All Dad had to do was wait. The night came. With Alfie driving, they followed Evans's crew to the jeweller's, then sat it out until the moment was right. The opportunity came when Evans and Marks walked past Dad's car. Alfie rolled out and drove up behind them slowly.

Dad wound down his window and called Marks's name. As Ginger stopped and turned, Dad emptied his

.38 revolver. Ginger went down straight away, but Evans acted quickly and used Ginger's body as a shield until he had the chance to make a run for it. Alfie gave chase, but Evans got away.

What happened didn't stop him coming back, though. A couple of days later, Evans and his firm returned to the scene of the crime to attempt the jewellery robbery again. Stupid bastard – he was the key witness to a murder inquiry, for fuck's sake. Little did he know it but he was under constant surveillance. Surprise, surprise, he and his crew got nicked.

Dad's firm were all questioned about Ginger's murder, but what they didn't know was that Evans had already snitched, naming Dad, Alfie, Jerry Callaghan and Ronnie as culprits. But the police hadn't enough evidence to arrest them. For one thing, they didn't have a body. But they all knew that Evans was scared. After all, he knew Freddie Foreman still wanted him dead. His fear sent him into self-preservation mode. The more public Evans made himself, the less likely anyone would be to touch him. He was happy to be featured in newspaper articles about the Marks murder: I've seen the photos of him pointing out bullet holes in the walls.

After being overheard boasting about it, Evans twice went to court accused of shooting my uncle George and possessing a firearm (which had been found in his home). He was acquitted both times. This might have had something to do with my uncle never agreeing to testify against Evans, but my dad suspected Evans got off because he was cooperating with the police, possibly over the Marks murder.

The police had their suspicions about Dad's involvement with Marks, but others were suspected too, and Dad never got nicked for it. Three years later, in 1968, Dad was arrested for Mitchell and McVitie and given his ten years.

In 1972, Evans was charged with the murder of William Fernie, a Scottish carpenter. The bloke had nothing to do with the underworld: he was doing nothing more than mucking about with a few mates, surrounding the car of Evans's common-law wife, Anick Webb. For this, Evans decided to stab Fernie and he died instantly. He beat the murder charge but got seven years for manslaughter in 1973. While Evans was on remand, the police asked him further questions about the Marks affair, and my dad is convinced that this was the time he struck a concrete deal with them. We all are. Maybe it's a coincidence that Evans served only three of his seven years and happened to be the key witness in the Ginger Marks inquiry, but somehow I doubt it.

Evans is a grass and he'll die a grass. It's thanks to him – and only him – that my uncle George nearly died, and that my dad was suddenly facing a trial that could rob him of his freedom for life. Evans was prepared to sacrifice the liberty of other men to save his own skin, and it's disgusting, pure and simple.

I was devastated when Mum told me that Dad had been charged. The dark clouds were back again. All the optimism I'd had about him getting out vanished and I was left with a feeling of pure dread. I was old enough to know what a life sentence meant – 15 years minimum. How the fuck was I – how the fuck were any of us – going to cope with that? That we might lose Dad again felt like the sickest joke in the world.

But I didn't go to pieces. None of us did. The news of the charge and the impending trial took a terrible toll on us, but we held it together. Sitting around depressed has no value in such a situation. There are times when you have to keep going; you have to fight tooth and nail against the demons in your head and keep moving forward. I was older now. I'd been through this before, and now I'd do it again, and do it better.

I'd be lying if I said my dad being accused of murder didn't bother me. It did, but only at first. After all, I had never heard of Ginger Marks, and didn't understand what had occurred. But once everything was explained to me and I understood why my father had taken a certain course of action, I can honestly say I had no conscience to wrestle with. If that sounds bad, so be it. I knew that Dad did what he did for a reason, and a good reason at that. My father is my father, and I know he has never – and would never – take unjustified action against another man. That's why I would stand by my dad no matter what.

Dad was moved from the Scrubs to Wandsworth, and we went to visit him at the first opportunity. There he was with that same old wink and a smile.

'It's all a get-up,' he said. 'We'll beat this, don't you worry. They haven't got anything.'

Knowing what he knew, Dad must have been sick with worry, but he didn't let on for a second. As always, he was a pillar of strength in front of me and Mum. Even so, there were things we needed to discuss. The cogs for building his defence needed to be set in motion, but we couldn't say a thing thanks to two screws noting down every word we said.

'Is this how it's going to be?' said Dad, looking at the screws.

''Fraid so, Fred. This is what we've been told to do.'

'Well, fuck this then.'

Dad turned to us. 'Listen, don't bother coming back here. I've only got a few more months and then they're going to move me to Brixton on remand. We'll get proper open visits there, so let's save it till then, eh?'

Mum agreed; me too. Desperate as I was to see Dad and help in any way, being glared at by a bunch of nosy screws made it impossible. We said our goodbyes and left. Anyway, there was plenty to be done on the outside. The machine went to work, as it had done for Dad's previous trials.

The committal came around – a hearing to decide whether the case went to trial or not. It was my first time in court and I'll never forget what it felt like seeing Dad and his firm entering the room. Alfie, Ronnie and Jerry walked in and stood in the dock, and then my dad was brought in, handcuffed to two of the biggest screws you've ever seen. Dad flashed us a smile as he sat down in front of the three chaps. So strong, so relaxed: Dad's demeanour was formidable. The accused all nodded to each other as proceedings began.

Chalk and Troon, the two coppers who had interviewed Dad in Wormwood Scrubs, got up to say their bit first. Referring to their interview notes, the officers began by asserting that, when questioned about Ginger Marks and Jimmy Evans, my father had called Evans a 'git' and said, 'One of these days I'll shut him up for good.' This was supposed to prove a link between Dad and Ginger.

Now, people from my father's world may use many strong words, but 'git' is not one of them! It's such a police word – the kind of thing you hear on telly – and I've never heard it used by anyone from my neck of the woods. The idea that Dad would have used 'git' in reference to a bloke who'd just grassed him up is laughable, let alone saying that he'd 'shut someone up for good' to two policemen. As soon as the cozzers opened their mouths, it was obvious to anyone who knew my dad that their evidence was unconvincing. But there was nothing we could do about it. Not yet, anyway.

Evans stood up and said a few words.

Another witness was brought in. His name was Smith, and Evans had solicited him to give evidence against Dad. He took the stand, and what happened next blew me away. Just before the hearing I'd been introduced to a bloke named Harry, who was there with us. He'd looked very pumped up but I thought nothing of it as we took our seats in the gallery. It wasn't until the prosecutor, Mr Matthews, began to question Smith that the penny dropped. Smith kept looking towards the gallery, his eyes directed at Harry. Every time Smith looked up, I saw Harry slowly shaking his head. It turned out that Harry was Smith's brother. Harry was a friend of my dad's, and it was just like the scene in *The Godfather* when they bring the old boy from Sicily over. Needless to say, Smith reneged on his statement. So, right away we'd managed to cut one bit of evidence off at the knees. He was a good man, Harry. We are still close to his family, God rest his soul.

With one witness down I felt a glimmer of hope that the case might not go to trial. Wishful thinking, really. The judge committed my dad, Alf, Ronnie and Jerry to trial several months down the line at the Old Bailey. Shattering news.

I looked at Dad as he was led towards the door and prayed there would be a way out of this. He still looked calm and collected, but suddenly everything changed. As Dad was about to pass Chalk and Troon, he yanked at his handcuffs and lurched forwards, bringing the two screws with him until he was level with the two policemen. He was wild with rage.

'You fucking satisfied now?' he yelled. 'Fitting us up, you no-good fucking cunts.'

The rest of the chaps had a go too. Alfie verballed the life out of them, screaming every name under the sun; Ronnie said his piece; and, last but not least, Jerry Callaghan spat in the faces of the shaken, terrified coppers.

It was an incredible scene – my dad's firm were doing things you just *don't do* to the police. I had never seen anything like it. They never took a backward step with anyone. What a firm!

Ten months, I thought. Ten months until my father defends himself in the trial of a lifetime. When we'd thought he was going to come out early, ten months seemed nothing. Now, with the worry that he might be given a life sentence, it felt like an age away. There would be dark days ahead, but there was nothing for it but to push on through and do everything possible to help Dad out of this.

My dad was a big scalp for the police to have. We knew how badly they wanted their pound of flesh, and that the prosecution would try every trick in the book to get it. Dad's defence would need to be equally clever, and watching the chaps and the lawyers build it was a lesson in pulling out all the stops. We didn't know exactly what evidence they had, so inducing doubt in the jury was the aim. What possible reason would

Freddie Foreman have to do such a thing to a man he never knew? What proof was there he wasn't alive? Where was the body? Why was Jimmy Evans making accusations against my father, when Evans himself was a convicted felon, a dishonourable human being?

When Dad's sentence was up, he was moved from the draconian Wandsworth Prison back to Brixton, where he joined Alfie, Ronnie and Jerry, who were already there on remand. Brixton was where it had all begun, all those years earlier. It must have been a terrible feeling for Dad to find himself back where he'd started. What strength it must have taken to dig deep, to say to himself, 'Right, I'm going to beat this. I'm not going to crack. I'm going to fight.'

And fight they did. From their cells they put together a killer defence. Ingeniously, Dad organised one of the chaps on the outside to break into Jimmy Evans's home and obtain a letter Evans had written to his girlfriend. Evans had been on remand when he wrote the letter and it contained an admission that made it pretty clear what the bastard was up to: 'I have sold my soul to the devil to be with you.' By the devil he meant the police, and that one sentence just about said it all. Copies were made and tucked away safely until the time came for the letter to be produced in court, and Jimmy the grass was none the wiser.

Now Dad was in Brixton we were able to visit without being spied on the whole time. Most days the chaps had a visit from one of the wives, who'd bring them food to keep their spirits up. In those days prisoners on remand were allowed to have their own food brought in – you were allowed to retain a lot more dignity. During the week the wives would cook nice healthy food for their husbands and friends, but on Sundays it was my turn. It gave the wives a break, and seeing as we only lived in Dulwich, a 15-minute drive away, it was no problem for me to do the cooking and drop it in for the chaps. On my day they got what they really loved – hearty stodge like steak, eggs, grilled tomatoes, mushrooms, beans and chips. They told me it was their favourite meal of the week. I'd get up at the crack of dawn to prepare whatever meals the chaps had ordered. Once I'd crammed as much as I could on their tin plates, I covered each meal with an upside-down plate and wrapped it in a knotted tea towel to keep everything warm. The funny thing was that it didn't matter how I presented the food, because when I turned up with it the screws invariably opened up every meal, scraped it on to a new plate and poked it about to check I wasn't bringing anything else in. Understandable, I suppose – a skeleton key smuggled in among the baked beans might have come in handy.

I loved helping out with those meals, but a thousand hot dinners couldn't change the fact that Dad was in danger, and the pressure took its toll on all of us. It's a private pain that you deal with as best you can. You think you're better off without anyone knowing. You think other people don't understand, nor do you want them to. But everyone found out, of course, because from the moment Dad was charged the story had been all over the papers. Nothing surprising about that – such a high-profile case is a licence to print money as far as the 'red tops' are concerned – but Dad being splashed across the front pages gave me another headache to deal with: my new friends at Conti's.

Since the incident at the school gates, my classmates had some idea who Dad was, that his was a name not to be trifled with, but it ended there. There was no reason for them to dwell on where their mate Jamie came from, and life went on uneventfully. But, once the news broke, all of my new mates suddenly knew a whole lot more about Dad, what he'd been up to in the past and what he was being accused of now. Not for one second have I ever been ashamed of my father or my background, but I did worry that what was being said – much of it twisted and untrue – would shock people into thinking twice about the Jamie they thought they knew. After all, I was mixing with a lot of people who had no understanding of the world I came from, and naturally I didn't want them to judge my father, my family or me from what they read in the newspapers.

Did the new people in my life demonise me and my family? Did they turn their backs on me? Quite the opposite. It turned out I didn't need to worry about a thing. For a start, I was at stage school, and should have realised that students at stage school are there out of a love for one thing – drama! I was overwhelmed by how supportive everyone was, not least the girls, who were very protective of me. If there was anything about that terrible period that you could call good, it was the 'sympathy' I received from some of those girls – and I won't mention any names!

Looking back, I think one of the reasons people treated me so kindly during that awful time was because I had only ever conducted myself well. I was always kind and gracious at Conti's – and elsewhere besides – and earned a lot of respect and goodwill from those I was close to. So when the *merde* hit the fan, there was nothing terrible about me anyone could reflect on and say, 'Ah, *now* we understand why he's that way' – I hope not anyway. In the months leading up to my father's trial, the kindness of others provided an occasional, brief oasis of relief from all the angst and misery. And I learned a lesson there – while people can't always understand what you're going through, they can offer solace, a sympathetic ear and sometimes a shoulder to cry on. Whatever happens in life, we're not meant to be alone in this world.

Summer drew to a close and as the nights grew darker the trial loomed ever closer. After what seemed like an age, November 1975 came, and with it began the trial at the Old Bailey, a building that to me seemed designed to put the fear of God into any mortal. I'll never forget the feeling of walking through its marble halls and hoping against hope that the prosecution weren't going to pull something out of the bag that would send Dad down. As things stood, we had a hunch that most of the evidence against Dad might be a little flimsy. Still, a supposed eyewitness was an extreme cause for concern.

Jimmy Evans was up as the first witness for cross-examination. The prosecution fed him all the right questions to ensure he blurted out every last detail about Ginger's murder and, true to the nature of a grass, he added a wealth of outrageous exaggeration to his testimony. Listening to him lying his arse off was enough to make you sick with rage. I'm sure Dad was boiling up inside, but he didn't show it. Instead he did something very clever. Right the way through Evans's little performance, Dad put on a much better one of his own. At perfectly timed moments, he shook his head, shrugged his shoulders in disbelief or let out a despairing tut – nothing over the top, nothing that would upset the judge, just enough for the jury to observe him and think twice about what they were listening to.

Dad was fighting for his life using every possible tactic, and acting was one of them. The theatricality of the scene, the subtle way Dad played the jury, was as good as anything I'd seen at the National. In a TV interview years later, Terry Wogan asked me if there was any acting in my family and I said, 'Yes, my father in the dock at the Old Bailey!' Terry liked that and laughed uproariously.

Next, Evans had to answer to the great Lewis Hawser QC, who was leading the defence team, an impressive array of the top defence QCs in the country. First off, Hawser made short work of squeezing Evans into admitting he had lied under oath during his own trial and at a divorce hearing. As you can imagine, this went down a treat with the jury, and wound Evans up no end.

Then it was time for the trump card: Evans's 'sold my soul' letter to his girlfriend. When the letter was produced, Hawser asked Evans if he would read out the damning passage. You could almost feel the blood draining from Evans's face – he was apoplectic with rage. 'How did you get that letter?' he screamed.

'Are you all right, Mr Evans?' asked Hawser. 'Would you like a glass of water? Clerk, would you hand Mr Evans a glass of water, please.'

'I don't want a glass of fucking water. I want to know where you got the letter. Those men did it. I swear on my life.'

It was very interesting watching a man known for his wild temper coming unglued, and better still when he suddenly lost it completely and tore up the letter. When it came to looking totally unreliable, Evans was doing an excellent job. All we had to do was sit back and watch.

Hawser probably could have left it there, but he came back for more. A tall man with an air of real gravitas about him, his deep, powerful voice and calm way of expressing himself reminded me of seeing Laurence Olivier at work. Here was a master in action, and his next question was perfectly timed to make sure Evans kept up the good work of looking like the unsavoury wretch he is. Aware of Evans's obsession with guns, he asked him to talk about the firearms used in the case.

Evans fell for it hook, line and sinker. Going well beyond the call of duty, he rabbited on uninterrupted about his fixation with weapons until the jury looked positively worried. Talk about – excuse the pun – shooting yourself in the foot. By the time he shut up, it was obvious to everyone that, at best, Evans had a few screws loose. No further questions, your honour.

By no means were we popping corks, but we definitely had a feeling that things weren't looking good for the prosecution. I remember allowing myself to dream that Dad was going to beat this, but all I could do was wait.

After several more days of legal toing and froing, it was time for the Chalk and Troon Show to begin in Court Number One. I don't want to sound flippant about a matter that was so serious – a feeling of dread never left me all the way through the trial – but, looking back, what happened when the police officers took the stand was pretty farcical. This result was once again down to Lewis Hawser, who was ready to deliver another crushing blow to the prosecution.

Hawser cross-examined Detective Sergeant Troon

about the 'questionnaires' he and Chalk had given to Jerry Callaghan and Alfie Gerrard when they were arrested for Ginger Marks's murder: were both men interviewed on the same day? Yes. Was the date and time of interview written at the top of each man's questionnaire? Yes. Did the interviews take place on 8 January 1975? Yes. Fine. Calm and polite, Hawser asked Troon if he had his police diary with him. He did. Were the dates and times of the interviews noted in said diary? Indeed they were. How soon after the interviews? Half an hour.

Now came the thunderbolt. In the light of his answers Troon was asked to explain why the questionnaires were dated 6 January when the date of the interview was 8 January.

Silence.

Hawser repeated the question.

More silence.

The tension in the courtroom was indescribable. Troon was totally stumped. It was obvious to judge and jury that they were looking at two very misleading, and very embarrassed, coppers.

No more questions.

The prosecution had brought a totally flawed case. They hadn't been able to prepare a good case because, quite simply, they didn't have one. Once Chalk and Troon stood down there was an electricity in the court that made me start to believe proceedings were really breaking down. Papers shuffled, lawyers whispered and murmured, and there was a disturbed air in the room, a subdued commotion. Things were not going to plan. Nothing was turning out as the authorities had hoped.

After a few minutes, Judge Donaldson sent the jury to wait outside so that the lawyers could argue among themselves. In the ensuing debate, I didn't understand half of the legal terms – it was like watching a play without understanding the words – but from body language alone I could tell something crucial was going down. Halfway through, I noticed Dad and Alfie looking at each other and nodding very slowly, almost gravely, at what was being said. As usual, they had poker faces, but a tiny glimmer in their eyes told me they knew something I didn't and that, whatever they knew, it was good.

Eventually, the lawyers fell silent and the judge asked for the jury to be called back in. He had something to say. Due to the way the evidence had been presented, and due to the lack of substantial evidence, he told the jury he had no alternative other than to direct them to find the men not guilty.

Not guilty. *Not guilty!*

At that moment they sounded like the most beautiful words in the world. Pure, overwhelming elation shot through me. We'd won. My dear, beloved father was free.

I'll never forget that dreamlike moment. The relief on everyone's faces said it all. I took Mum's hand – we didn't need to say a word – and together we gazed down at Dad, who beamed back at us. It was over, and I felt like my whole body was smiling.

We were magnanimous in victory, as was Dad. Justice had been done, but there was no screaming or shouting from the gallery, no cheering or jumping for joy. Rubbing people's noses in it wasn't the way we did things. After giving us a quiet thumbs up, Dad graciously bid farewell to the prosecution lawyers, thanked his team, Judge Donaldson and, last but not least, the jury.

For all those years, I had visited Dad in prison, and I was so used to the pain of watching him being led away from me that, even though he had won, I felt the usual – habitual – pang of sadness and loss as he was led out of court. My brain hadn't yet rewired itself to believe that my father was free. Images of those horrible visits to Leicester flashed through my mind, and for just a couple of seconds I was gripped by a strange fear that he still wasn't coming back to us, that they'd find a way to hold on to him. Christ, I thought, the things we've been through. I took one more look at the courtroom, turned my back and walked out.

I noticed Chalk and Troon as I descended the grand old stairs of the Old Bailey. They were standing in the hall like a couple of lemons, all sheepish and embarrassed, and I had to really fight the urge to front up to them. I wanted to laugh in their faces, spit in their eyes. *Fuck you!* I thought. *Fuck both of you.* I wanted to say it to them, but I didn't. I wasn't brought up that way. When I caught their eyes, I just nodded politely and smiled.

Outside, the press were on us like vultures. Cameras snapped and journalists crammed around us hoping for comment. Giving them a soundbite was the last thing on our minds, especially since the papers had never given us an easy ride in the past. I did my best to protect Mum from them as we waited for Dad to emerge from the building.

Everyone congratulated one another on the pavement, and I remember my mother's hand shaking with emotion. I can't speak for her, but there was a worry in the back of my mind: the last time Dad had beaten a murder rap – the Frank Mitchell case – he'd immediately been charged with the McVitie job. Although I knew there was paperwork to be dealt with before Dad could be released, a part of me dreaded they would be sticking something else on him while we stood there waiting. No one knows what goes on behind closed doors, and I wouldn't be satisfied until the doors of the Old Bailey opened and my dad walked out of them.

We waited and waited. Then, all of a sudden, someone let out a cry.

'Here he is!'

Everyone spun round and, sure enough, there he was. Freddie Foreman. *My father*.

Dad looked fantastic in his navy-blue Savile Row suit. Needless to say, he was very happy, but Dad has never been a flamboyant man, and as he took his first steps of freedom there was a dignity to him that I will never forget. He was able to carry himself with such quiet composure, each step taking him further away from the injustice and suffering of all those years, each stride bringing him closer to his loved ones.

And then we were in his arms, together again, the way it was meant to be. I can't tell you how good – how right – that moment felt. I began to tremble as he held me tight. For a few seconds it was as if nothing else existed or mattered. It was as if an anvil had been lifted from my shoulders. It's strange, but, when you have carried a huge amount of stress for so many years, it's not until it has been lifted that you truly realise what a toll it has taken on you.

'Hello, Fred, I'm from the *Sunday People*...' brought the situation sharply back into focus. There we were trying to enjoy a moment of fresh air together for the first time in nearly a decade, and some hack was trying to get a story. Dad turned his head in the direction of the voice and, just as the journo was about to ask a question, cut him short.

'Oh yes, I remember *you*,' said Dad very quietly, the smile disappearing from his face. Alf was at his shoulder, growling. I don't know what Dad remembered, but it can't have been good, for he fixed his eyes on the reporter and gave him the look of all looks. In an instant, the man's face turned ashen and he shrivelled into the background. Then, as if a switch had been flicked, Dad was all smiles again. Even in those moments of heightened emotion, of triumph, he wasn't letting anything, or anyone, get past him. Freddie Foreman was back, and it was glorious.

Finally it was time to enjoy ourselves. We all jumped in taxis and headed over to the A & R Club. I was already well acquainted with the place, having delivered numerous 'messages' to and from Mick Regan, while my dad was being held on remand. I'll never forget a visit to Brixton one day when Dad told me to deliver a message. It was the first time I had felt useful and important and trusted. Little did I know it wouldn't be the last time the firm used my help; nor could I have guessed where that responsibility would eventually lead me.

The A & R was the place all the chaps used to congregate, and I'll never forget the moment we arrived that afternoon. Dad and Uncle Mick had always been close, but Mick had been put away before Dad in the sixties, so they hadn't seen each other in a very long time. At first they didn't say a word, but simply looked at each other. You could tell how close they were from the way they stopped still. They'd been through so much together, and there was so much love between them. Like brothers, really.

In those days men in our world always greeted each other by shaking hands. It was the old-fashioned way. Men hugging is a relatively recent convention, but back then a firm handshake sufficed. Most of the time, anyway. On this occasion, after a few more seconds of standing there, Uncle Mick broke the silence and stretched his arms out. 'I don't give a fuck what they'll say,' he boomed, and gave Dad a hug and a kiss. Seeing the reunion of those two great men was a beautiful moment.

The club was quiet at first, but, as word got around, more and more people showed up to celebrate and pay their respects to Dad. By early evening the place was packed. I knew a fair few of the friends and family in the room, but there were many more faces I didn't recognise. After all, I had been just ten when Dad had gone away, and back then I only had vague notions about the world he was moving in. Now I was an adult, witnessing hundreds of men congregating in my father's name – major robbers and chaps, a *Who's Who* of the London scene – and it was a real eye-opener. In his absence, I'd heard many a conversation about what a major player Dad was, and now I was witnessing it for myself. What a spectacle – it really made you square your shoulders and stick your chin out with pride.

It was a strange and wonderful afternoon. In some ways I felt as if nothing had changed – Dad was with us, surrounded by those he loved, and making plans – but in other ways it was as if everything had changed. I was no longer a little boy running around the pub being kissed by the women. Now I was an adult and suddenly I felt a part of everything. The chaps treated me as one of their own, and I had a tremendous sense that I belonged in an adult world I had nothing but respect for. The question was: how would Dad react to me doing adult things he disapproved of? I would find out that very afternoon.

Dad had always been a non-smoker, but while he'd been away I'd taken up the habit. Mum knew it, Ronnie Knight too, but Dad didn't have a clue. It was the only secret I'd ever kept from him. Not wanting to upset him, I'd gone the whole afternoon without a cigarette, and I was gasping for one. Ronnie clocked me squirming and kindly brought the subject up with Dad.

'Fred, I think there's something Jamie wants to tell you, and not being honest with you is getting to him.'

Dad was all ears.

'I've got to tell you, Dad,' I said, a touch nervous. 'I smoke and I'm dying for a cigarette.'

Dad was hardly pleased – what sort of father would be? – yet he didn't get angry or lay down the law.

'Standing there not having one must have been killing you,' he said, smiling. 'I'm not happy, but go on then.'

Dad had always been fair and, small as it may seem, that moment confirmed nothing was going to change on that front now he was home. I had grown up, and Dad fully accepted it. He wasn't holding on to the idea of the boy I'd been the last time he was free, and the nature of that little exchange was a blueprint for the way our relationship would continue. We were both men now.

Day became night, and the gathering turned into a true London occasion filled with music, laughter and singing. I didn't let Dad out of my sight, and stood by his side nearly every moment of that joyous reunion. Now I had him back, I didn't want to let him go for a second.

At one point I relaxed a little, stood back from Dad's group and watched him work the room. It felt almost unreal to have him back again, to see him smiling and talking as if the past seven years were merely a bad dream he'd forgotten instantly. Those years haven't changed him one iota, I thought. They hadn't broken him one bit.

We had a proper good drink with all the right people. As the night went on, there were groups of men huddled around each other, Dad included, their conversation hushed. They say business and pleasure don't mix, but on this night that didn't apply. There was business to be done, meets to be planned. Arrangements were being made. Lumps of cash were already exchanging hands. My dad was ready to go back to work with his firm. Freddie Foreman was already back in business.

The man of the house was home, but, when we woke up the following morning, Dad was nowhere to be seen. 'Where's Daddy?' I said to Mum when I got downstairs. Before she had a chance to shrug her shoulders, our answer walked through the front door.

'Help me get some things in from the car, Jamie,' said Dad with a grin.

I gladly obliged. Just hearing something so mundane was music to my ears. Being there to help my dad at home felt wonderful. The next thing I knew we were hauling in bags and boxes filled with a ton of gorgeous food. I'd done a similar thing for Mum while Dad was away, but this was different – Dad had really gone to town and bought every goody a family could hope for. Enough to last for weeks.

It turned out that, when he'd woken up, Dad had gone to the fridge and the cupboards and found them pretty bare, and I think that moment had hit him hard. It symbolised how much we'd sacrificed while he was away. Even though we were living in a beautiful house with beautiful furniture – all the outward trappings of wealth – there hadn't been an awful lot of money in the purse for living. A lovely place to live doesn't mean a lot if the cupboards are nearly empty.

Mum and I had always put a brave face on during visits, and never let Dad know about our dire financial worries – there was no value in making him feel worse about a situation he couldn't help. Besides, Dad had always done everything he could for us even when he was inside. I vividly remember one visit not long after he had been moved to the Scrubs. We had barely sat down when Dad told Mum to take his hand. She reached across the table, her eyes darting towards the guards. I surreptitiously clocked what he put in her hand before it disappeared into her handbag. It was 50 quid. 'I'll give you the same every visit, and someone will be in touch. He'll be dropping more round to you,' he told her.

How had Dad got his hands on that kind of money in prison? I wondered. What was he up to? What had he set up? He must have read my mind, for he looked at me and winked. 'I'm back in London now,' he said, as if it was all that needed saying, as if the walls that had incarcerated him were inconsequential. Mum and I went for a spag on the way home and, when I asked her how he got the money, she just looked at me and smiled. 'Ask no questions, get told no lies. That's your dad. That's what he's like. I gave up asking questions a long time ago.'

Sure, we'd survived, but those bags stuffed with food were Dad's way of saying the difficult days were over. He'd found it hard to deal with how much we'd sacrificed, and his reaction was so touching. An unspoken acknowledgement of our pain and a thank you for having gone through it with dignity. Nothing was ever lost on Dad, and even now that tender moment brings a tear to my eye.

It was a joy to have Dad home, and a sense of profound relief at having my father where he belonged stayed with me for days. It might sound odd, but I still feel that relief now. When someone has been absent from your life for so long, when life has felt *wrong* for so long, every day feels like a blessing from the moment things are right again. Even during testing moments, you cast your mind back to how bad life has been, thank your lucky stars it all turned out OK and stop moaning before you start. It's an attitude I've applied to other areas of life, especially acting. It always winds me up when I hear actors moaning while they're working. A common complaint is 'I'm so bored sitting around on set all day', and hearing it from an actor drives me mad. I just want to tell them to think about all the years they've been lying on the sofa waiting for the phone to ring, the dozy fools.

9

DAD AND ME

Now I had my father back, I didn't want to let him go. There was so much lost time to make up for, and I wanted to be with him constantly. And I knew the feeling was mutual. Still, I knew Dad needed to earn a living and, knowing where his way of life had landed him before, I was nervous about the prospect of him going back to work. One night, just after he was back, Dad and I had a conversation and our feelings came out.

'I'm so proud of you, Jamie,' said Dad. 'You've been so brave for so long, and you've looked after your mother. You've been the man of the house, and now it's time for you to enjoy yourself.'

Kind, moving words.

'I know things have been hard,' he continued. 'But I'll soon have a bit of work lined up. We'll be back on top in no time, you'll see.'

Don't say that, I thought. Dad was being so considerate to me and it was really appreciated, but the mention of 'jobs' made my heart sink. I'd just got him home, and I couldn't bear the idea of my dear father getting done for something and being taken away from us again. I didn't need to speak – my face must have said it all. I'll never forget what he said next.

'Jamie, I know what you're thinking, but, if I don't go back to work, they win. They would have beaten me, and no one beats me. I've had seven years taken from me, and I know it's been hard on you all. But I need you to understand that I have to show them I'm still the man I was.'

I understood. For Dad, going back to work was a matter of necessity. He belonged to a certain part of society – a world that had defined him his entire life – and leaving it would have been like waving goodbye to his identity. For good or for bad, he would always be the man he was, and Dad's words made me realise that it was a matter of self-esteem and pride. Asking my father to change his ways would have been like asking for a new dad, and I loved him exactly as he was. Just as he had been supportive of whatever I wanted to do – he loved the fact I was building an acting career for myself – I would have to accept and support the choices he made. Were it not for him, I would never have had so many opportunities given me in the first place. You can't ask someone to change without compromising your relationship, and I'd rather have died than done that. At the end of the day, family is about accepting each other for who you all are, and it was the least I could do for my father.

What's more, accepting Dad's choices was made easier because I understood the appeal of the underworld. I loved my fledgling career as an actor and everything that went with it, but I also found my dad's lifestyle seductive and exciting. Depending where you are in the hierarchy of the criminal world, it can be a fascinating, dangerous and thrilling feeling. When you're in the basement, it's an unpleasant, seedy place, but experience it at the top echelons and there's an undeniable buzz that's hard to beat. There's intrigue, money, drama, danger and power – elements that, good or bad, make you feel truly alive – and I must admit I liked being on the periphery of something that most people never experience close up. I'll make no excuses for that.

Dad never wanted me to follow in his footsteps, and I had no intention of doing so. I was beginning to make a name for myself acting, and had started to nick some nice jobs on children's TV. But, as I've said, Dad and I were desperate to be together as much as possible, so it ended up that whenever I wasn't working we would spend time together. Being with him meant being in his environment, and it suited me just fine. I'd already dipped my toe in parts of London's underworld, and the prospect of wading in a little further didn't bother me one bit. In fact, I loved being by my father's side. It was the adventure – and education – of a lifetime.

Dad had to rebuild his life. Apart from the house, all of his assets – the pub, various betting shops and other properties – had been sold before or while he served his time. It's fair to say that before he went away he was a very wealthy man, but the cost of hiring the best legal minds doesn't come cheap. After so many years away, he had to go back to grass roots. He was out and he was hungry.

Dad cast his net wide. He reassembled all of his old contacts, and with Fred back in circulation it wasn't long before he was being offered 'business' – the odd share in a club or a pub in an unsavoury part of town where his name would ensure there was no trouble. And friends who were having trouble in reclaiming money owed, who for one reason or another didn't want to go to the authorities, would come to him, and he would see what he could do. He always seemed to be able to work something out in exchange for a nice 'drink' out of what he got back for them. And then, most importantly of all to him, there was his preferred line of work out on the pavement. I can't go into details here, but, suffice it to say, Dad didn't waste much time in proving to himself he still had what it takes to be a fine money-getter.

As often as I could, I was there to drive my father wherever he needed to be. I wouldn't be burned off. The only times he'd leave me behind was for my own good. To keep me out of danger. If Dad was going on a meet where having my face on show would implicate me unnecessarily, he'd make sure I was out of the picture. But, wherever we went, my eyes kept opening wider – the flavour of Dad's world I'd had before was nothing compared with what I witnessed in this period. Day after day, it never ceased to amaze me how many people Dad met with and how many places we'd get around. There was never a pattern. In one day alone I might drive Dad to a meet at an Eton Square mansion, or an apartment in Regent's Park covered in Picasso paintings, then to a smoky little drinking club, then to a beautiful restaurant and on to a spieler before a meeting in an East End pub. Constantly Dad met with an incredible diversity of people. From important high-society gents to men whose lives were played out in the murkiest corners of the underworld, I was introduced first hand to a London of contrasts I'd so far only scraped the surface of.

Every meeting was a different bit of business, but most of the time I had little idea of the details. You've all heard the phrase 'I'm just the driver' – well, nine times out of ten it applied to me. While Dad loved having me with him, there was no way he wanted to drag his son into anything incriminating. With me, and anyone else in his firm, Dad operated on a strictly need-to-know basis.

Many times I'd wait in the car, but, on any meets I did get to sit in on, I learned to keep my ears shut and act as if I wasn't there. It goes without saying that whatever I knew about Dad's business I never passed on.

Dad was a smooth operator, always in total control. As we drove around I could always sense him thinking about where we had been and where we were going next. At first he would always remind me not to tell the next person where we'd come from or what we'd been up to. To arrive at a meeting and even say the area of London we'd travelled from was taboo. If I had to make a phone call I wasn't to use names: it was never 'Hello, it's Jamie, Fred's on his way' but simply 'We're on our way' and down with the receiver. I learned the importance of keeping my mouth shut about everything, and it soon became second nature.

One of Dad's favourite meeting spots was known as 'bacon sandwiches', my Auntie Nanette's place in Kennington Road, so called because the first thing Auntie Nanette – or 'Nanny' as we called her – said when you walked in was: 'Fancy a bacon sandwich?' The chaps loved to congregate there, and meets at Nanny's were often a good chance for Dad to have a proper catch-up with one of the firm he'd been keeping a low public profile with. I'll never forget my feeling of surprise when we turned up at Nanny's one day and sitting there was a bloke I'd noticed in the pub the night before. He'd been sitting in the corner while I had been drinking with Dad, but they might as well have been strangers – they hadn't even acknowledged each other. Now the same fellow was drinking a cup of tea, eating a doorstep sandwich and asking us how our night went. Then he and Dad got down to business. I was always thrilled at the amount of subterfuge in Dad's world: you never knew who was linked to whom, or when you were going to have your assumptions challenged.

Dad had connections that opened doors and earned you favours everywhere. His name even had its uses among the police, and I learned this in a rather amusing way. I drove around in a Hillman, a lovely little motor that I'd put in my mum's name as I didn't have a licence. One day the police pulled me over and held me up because I couldn't produce the right documents. Worried about getting Mum into trouble, I gave the name of a bloke I knew from the Borough. He'd passed his test, so my thinking was I could go down the station later on and use his licence. Little did I know they were going to nick me there and then. I ended up spending Friday night in Manor Place Police Station, off Walworth Road, roasting in a cell while everyone else was out and about. They kept asking me to repeat my name, and I kept sticking up the false one. In the meantime, they sent some officers round to my mate's address and, lo and behold, he'd just got back from the pub, gone to the door with a kebab in his hand and answered to the name I'd given the police. 'Thank you very much. Sorry to bother you,' said the police before making their way back to the station.

Before I knew it, my cell door swung open and three very angry police officers and an irate desk sergeant were leaning over me, fists clenched. 'You lying little fucker,' said the sergeant. 'If you're who you say you are, then you're at home with a kebab!'

The jig was up. I was gutted. It was time to come clean.

'All right,' I sighed, 'my name is Jamie Foreman.'

'What – Freddie's son?'

I nodded.

'Well, why didn't you fucking say so? You'd have been out of here five hours ago!'

Dad was called down to the station. When he saw me, he did a good job of acting angry, but only for the benefit of the police officers. 'You know your mother could get nicked, you taking her car without permission,' he shouted, making sure he gave me a wink while they weren't looking. A few minutes later I was out.

It turned out that if I'd given my name the police would have given me a 'producer' form, which gave you seven days to produce your documents. Because someone in Dad's firm always had a desk sergeant 'straight' somewhere, Dad would be able to pass the ticket on with a little something, usually a pony – £25. It would be entered in the book that you had 'produced' and that would be that.

It was a simple system, and on many a future occasion a desk sergeant earned more than a nice little drink out of me. Back in those days touches like that were one of the perks of being a desk sergeant. The money helped them out considerably with the wages they were on. Times have changed and they can't get away with it any more, which is a shame for both them and us. A harmless feature of a bygone era.

One day Dad was due to meet Buster Edwards – one of the Great Train Robbers and also my godfather – at his flower stall in front of Waterloo Station. I pulled up across the road and waited in the car while Dad went off. He'd only been gone a few minutes when the next thing I knew he was running back towards the car. Wondering what was going on, I started the engine. Dad jumped in and I pulled away sharpish.

'What's the matter?' I asked as we sped off.

'Just go around the block.'

I did as I was told, drove down to Stamford Street, round the block and back down Waterloo Road. Alongside Buster's pitch I saw a man lying unconscious on the pavement. A few confused passers-by were looking on. Dad looked on too, but there was no confusion on his part – it was him who'd knocked the bloke out. It was another case of Dad not being able to let a bully get away with it. The guy was a big, frightening lump who'd taken to walking up to local office workers, young men and women, shoving pens in their hands, and demanding money for them. Buster didn't like him, and had often told him to clear off, and by coincidence he'd shown up again at a time when Dad and Buster – two men with a hatred of liberty takers – were on a meet. Noticing him walking towards them, Buster explained the situation to Dad, and once again told the bloke to sling his hook. But the stupid bastard wasn't having any of it. Instead, he glared at my dad and asked him what the fuck he was looking at. Big mistake. With what Buster had told him adding fuel to his fire, Dad lured the bloke on and laid him spark out with one punch. Now, five minutes later, he was still out cold. We waited in the car until we were certain he had come around, then drove off. The bloke's pen-selling days were over, and he was never seen in the area again. I had to admire Dad for taking direct action against such an undesirable character.

The first time I really saw Dad go to work with his hands was on a night out at the Bloomsbury Centre. They were to hold a bareknuckle fight at the Continental Hotel, and on this occasion boxing legends Roy 'Pretty Boy' Shaw and Lenny 'The Guv'nor' McLean were about to go head to head. As it turned out, most of the night's action happened outside of the ring.

All the chaps were there. It was like the gathering of the clans, a roll-call of London's underworld, and the atmosphere was electric. It was intoxicating to walk into this almost Shakespearean environment and see my father being greeted with such respect, like he was a lord returning from the wars. We took our seats and waited for the gladiatorial champions to do battle: Roy Shaw was our man. The night was to decide who was the best street-fighter.

A couple of the early fights on the bill had already taken place when I began to sense that something wasn't quite right. People were coming to my father and passing messages; Dad wasn't watching the fights any more, and he and Ronnie Oliffe – seated at his side, just like the old days – were becoming agitated. I asked what all the fuss was about. Apparently, some months before, my uncle Fred had been involved in an altercation with a member of a good family from North London. There had been a fight outside the A & R. Fred had not known who this person was but it was clear there would be consequences. I loved Fred and his wife Jeanie, a beautiful woman and one of my favourite aunts. Fred unfortunately passed away several years ago. He had fought for his country in Malaysia with great distinction and is sorely missed. He was my mum's brother and had always been there for us while Dad was away. Ironically the person he had the run-in with, Roy, is now a very good friend of mine.

They were a strong firm who turned up that night, spotted my uncle Fred sitting near them and wanted to have a row with him there and then. But Ronnie Knight told Roy – who has the highest respect for Dad, as we do for him and his family – that Fred was Dad's brother-in-law, and not to take any action. The grievance would be sorted out amicably after the fights. This suited everyone, as neither side wanted any bad blood between them. But unfortunately some of the allies of the North London firm jumped the gun before they got Ronnie's message and attacked my uncle.

I saw it kick off across the ring.

'Dad, that's where Uncle Fred is sitting,' I said.

Dad leaped to his feet – Ronnie at his side, me behind – and we charged to my uncle's aid. Dad's entire firm followed right behind us. When we reached my uncle, Dad really went to work. I'd never seen it kick off on such a scale. I saw someone hit the deck, then another and then another.

In my life I've seen all kinds of violence – football violence, pub brawls, you name it – but when you see people who have grown up in the underworld, people who really know how to look after themselves and can *really* punch – it's something else.

Suddenly, this huge mass of a man was shaping up to my dad. He had ginger hair, he was six foot five and weighed in at around 17 stone. It was him who had started it all. Dad squared up to him.

'Do you want a bit of me?' said Dad.

'Come on then, I'll have some of you,' the guy growled back.

That was it. Dad glanced over the ginger man's

shoulder – a split-second distraction that just unsettled him – then stepped forward, threw a straight right and caught him right on the button. When the punch connected, it sounded like two trains shunting. The ginger guy's eyes hit the top of his head and he fell to the floor, ironing-board straight. He got some of Dad all right. What a punch!

There was fighting everywhere. My uncle Mick stood toe to toe with opponent after opponent before laying them out, and Dad and Ronnie Oliffe were dropping people left, right and centre. Watching Dad and Ron together was incredible. They'd fought off many challengers over the years and had their technique down to a fine art. There was a kind of telepathy between them – Dad attacking, Ron minding his back. It was carnage, like a saloon brawl in a cowboy movie. Chairs flew through the air and were being used as weapons. I must admit I used one myself to make sure that, once down, nobody got up. The finale came when my father pinned another big lump against a wall and pummelled him to the floor with fists and a chair.

When it was over, the scene looked like the aftermath of a battle. Bodies were strewn on the floor and my dad and his firm stood victorious. It had been a good old-fashioned 'straightener'. No knives, just fists and reputations. There was even a film crew – there to film the night's boxing – who captured the whole thing. I am clearly visible putting a chair about in that film.

People had climbed into the ring to escape the mêlée, and by the time it was over there were more people in the ring than out of it. Even Lenny McLean had got up there to keep himself out of harm's way – I think he knew there were a few people around who would have loved to have copped for him too. Roy Shaw had looked on and I remember him saying the punch Dad threw at the ginger guy was the best punch of the night. From a man as formidable as Roy, that's a true compliment.

The job was done, and the ginger guy's lot were in pieces all around the ring. Our firm left the devastation behind, and walked off quietly before the Old Bill showed up. We adjourned to a private club in Soho that Dad had a share in with Jimmy Hussey, one of the Great Train Robbers. Strange as it may sound, it wasn't until we got to the club that the adrenalin rush kicked in. The chaps were always calm when they went to work; the buzz came when the post-fight discussions began. There were a few sore heads, and a lot of laughter, as they bathed their cuts in the bathroom.

That night I saw Dad knock out four or five people, and I remember looking at him in awe and realising just how far he was prepared to go to set a situation straight. Another firm had taken a liberty with one of Dad's own, and justice had been done. I'm proud to say that I have never seen my father use violence where it wasn't called for, never seen him attack without cause, and for that I have nothing but respect. I make no attempt to romanticise what to most seems like a lawless and sometimes savage faction of society. I'm merely describing events and the attitudes of those who took and take part in them. Like it or loathe it, the world my dad moved in back then was as much a part of London life as any other.

After such huge clashes, comebacks are often on the cards. Dad made it perfectly clear to all concerned that he felt the matter was closed, and that anyone who felt differently would be dealt with swiftly and decisively. It seemed nobody wanted any more trouble, as we heard nothing more from the troublemakers. As it turned out, the family – whose 'friends' had jumped the gun without their consent – are very close to us now, and good friends.

The dust had settled and it was back to work as usual. Dad was grafting hard to build up funds again, and pretty soon a business opportunity came our way that, since it was totally legitimate, I was more than happy to get involved in. Thanks to a £10,000 investment from Micky Regan and Ronnie Knight, Dad and his close friend Ted Dennis were able to start a new venture.

Dad and Ted bought 60 pool tables and set about asking landlords all over London if they wanted a table in their pub. The deal was simple: we installed and maintained the tables, and collected the money from them fortnightly. The landlords received half the takings, and we took the rest – a straight-down-the-line, 50-50 arrangement. In addition to this, any pub with one of Fred's pool tables received protection from Dad – if the landlord had any trouble in his pub, Dad would sort it out.

It was the kind of thing people could call a protection racket, but in truth it was protection without the racket. Nobody was forced to take a table, but hardly any of the governors said no because they knew the value of having Dad's name associated with their pub. Those who said 'no thanks' were left be. In the end, we were taking phone calls from publicans all over London asking us if we'd put a table in, and I think that says a lot.

I loved helping Dad out with the pool rounds. The pool-table business was pretty new and proved very lucrative. Our collection rounds were meticulously organised – every collection route was planned around our stomachs! Where to stop for lunch was the question. One week it would be pie and mash at Cookes in the Cut at Waterloo, the next the Chop House in Farringdon Road or the Grange café in Grange Road near Tower Bridge. Soon we were making so much money that – thanks to machines jam-packed with 10p coins – we had to collect more and more often. Before we knew it takings had hit £3,000 a week, and Mick and Ronnie got their money back. Dad was making good legitimate money and everybody was happy. Apart from the police, that is.

One of our landlords phoned us saying that the police had come in and confiscated our pool table. This was closely followed by another call, then another. We were livid: the fucking police were messing with a bona fide business, but why? Once nicked, the tables were being stored at Camberwell Police Station. Someone was taking the piss, and that someone turned out to be our dear old friend DS Troon. It was almost too good to be true – or should I say *Troon*? He was back, this time in charge of an operation attempting to bring Dad's business to its knees.

Dad and his solicitor presented Troon with all the paperwork relating to the business, including shop receipts for all the pool equipment, and told him to reinstall the tables unless he wanted to face a charge of robbery. Not for the first time, Troon was lost for words and had to stand down. The tables were justly returned, and my father took great pleasure watching two exhausted, out-of-breath policemen straining under the massive weight of the tables as they moved them back to various pubs. Troon had taken another pot shot at Dad and missed. Oh how sweet revenge can be!

The pool-table business put enough money in our pockets for Dad to begin investing elsewhere. In partnership with his brother George, he acquired a bar in the Ellerslie Hotel (now called the Astral) at the top of Sydenham Hill in Crystal Palace. Originally we had been asked to come on board by an old friend, a lovely lady called Jan. The place had a lounge bar that we turned into a wonderful watering hole for after the pubs had shut every Sunday afternoon. My uncle George always made sure the complimentary roast potatoes were heavily salted – 'Makes 'em drink more,' he'd say. My brother Gregory worked the bar and I kept him stocked up, collected the glasses and schmoozed the punters. We had some great times up there. It wasn't long before – due to public demand – we were open Thursday, Friday and Sunday lunchtimes. We eventually turned the basement into a nightclub and it became a hot little venue. I was the DJ. Business boomed, and much later Dad ended up buying a share of the hotel and selling it for a tidy profit.

You might think that helping Dad out wouldn't have left much time to pursue acting, but far from it. Alongside my involvement with the family business, I was really cracking away and felt like my career was progressing nicely. Unfortunately, my work with the National had been over for a while, but what a great start it had been. That formative experience gave me the confidence to approach auditions with a 'if you don't like what you see, it doesn't bother me' attitude – that's the naivety of youth!

If I didn't get a part I could always spend more time with my dad, which I loved, but amazingly my approach to auditions seemed to be paying off. I was nicking almost every part I went for and, without wanting to blow my own trumpet, I do remember several occasions when I turned up to an audition only to hear a groan from the other hopefuls go round the room. All too often (for them, anyway!) it seemed I had the face that fitted the role, and I'm proud to say that sometimes I beat a few more well-known names to a part.

My success, I believe, was partly down to my being a good talker, and mature for my age. I never told lies or tried to say what I thought people wanted to hear: I was just myself, and directors seemed to lap it up. Not to say that I got everything, of course. One of the greatest lessons I've learned over the years is never to worry about what you don't get. Don't take it personally – if you don't have what they're looking for, there isn't much you can do about it, end of story. Be yourself, trust yourself, and sooner or later you'll walk into the right part. But always be prepared to give anything a go and push yourself, as sometimes the results will take even you by surprise.

I'll never forget the time I went for a part when the script stated 'six-foot, pretty, blond boy'. Now I am five foot eight, dark-haired and not all that pretty – more of a character actor's face. But I can't have been that bad-looking – I was once featured as a page-four 'Cor!' in a teenagers' weekly magazine. Anyway, I managed to turn heads at the audition and make them think about the role in a totally different way. I was more gobsmacked than any of the six-foot pretty boys must have been when it was announced I'd been picked for the part.

My first decent break came when I landed the role of

a young boy in a sweeping drama made by London Weekend Television called *Holding On*. I loved it. It was about the life of Charlie Wheelwright, an East End docker, played by Michael Elphick. The series covered Charlie's life from the age of nine until he was an old man – a span of 80 years. I played Charlie when he was 14 in 1913, and Michael took over once the character grew up. It was a convincing bit of casting because Michael and I did look pretty similar back then.

The script called for my Charlie to be seduced by a kept woman, played by the beautiful Lois Baxter. The day we did the bed scene was very nerve-racking. I was only about 17, she was topless and I was to lie in her arms. Her first line was 'They must feed you on raw meat' – very flattering.

There were about 40 people watching us, and I was pretty nervous and not used to being stared at in such compromising positions. Lois was great and handled the whole thing with wonderful dignity. She really helped me through it, and by the time we were done I was happy as Larry.

In another scene I had to kiss the lovely Linda Robson. But I cut up rough as I spot she's brought along her mate, played by Pauline Quirke. It was the first time I worked with the girls and we are still friends all these years later. They both went on to have great success with the hit sitcom *Birds of a Feather*.

I'd like to add that I was very sad when we lost

Michael Elphick to his terrible addiction to alcohol. He was a gentle and very sensitive man, and he really took me under his wing during the making of *Holding On*, and often took me to the best drinking holes frequented by the acting fraternity – my favourite was Jerry's Club in Shaftesbury Avenue. I would often get a little sozzled during rehearsals, much to the consternation of the producer, my old mate Paul Knight. Mike would tell Paul my condition wasn't his doing, and that I could drink him under the table, but I think Paul just despaired of the both of us. Mike had fantastic acting qualities. He had a strength, a gentleness, an everyman quality that made people feel safe when they were watching him. He found great popularity with *Boon*, although my favourite of his was the BBC's fantastic Second World War comedy series *Private Schulz*, written by Jack Pulman. If Mike could have only kicked the booze, he would have graced us with so much more. Thankfully we met up shortly before he died. We worked on a very lucrative voice-over for a major computer company, and afterwards went on to Jerry's club for a drink and a lovely long chat, just like old times. He told me he had followed my progress, which was lovely of him, and I had a chance to say goodbye.

Slowly but surely I began moving into more TV work. At one point I got a part in a Dick Emery sketch on his TV show. I was very excited – everyone loved Emery, who was about the biggest star at the BBC at the time. His primetime Saturday-night comedy programme regularly pulled in 15 million viewers. I made sure I knew all my lines, and turned up for the first day's rehearsal. I was pretty much word-perfect, but every time Emery forgot one of his lines he gave *me* a dirty look. Cheeky sod, I thought, but I stood for it the first day. He pulled the same stunt the second day, but I've never been anyone's whipping boy, and it wasn't long before I couldn't stand any more of it. Emery had just given me another look when I decided enough was enough.

'Excuse me,' I said. 'Why do you keep looking at me when you get your lines wrong? It ain't my fault. I know my lines.'

The next thing I know he's walking out of the room. The producer, Harold Snoad, called me into his office and tried to give me a dressing-down.

'You can't upset Mr Emery like that,' he said, terrified his big star had been offended.

'Fuck Mr Emery,' I said. 'I won't be made his whipping boy.' It was the first time anything like that had happened to me. 'Sack me if I've done anything wrong.' I didn't get the sack – we got on with it but Emery never spoke to me again. Mind you, he never spoke to anyone else in the cast either.

I also did a sketch in a *Two Ronnies* show. They were a different class, as were Morecambe and Wise – whenever you saw them they would smile and say hello.

But Emery wouldn't give you the time of day. He really burst that bubble and I didn't like him.

When I was about 18, I landed a lead role alongside the lovely and very talented Leslie Manville in a new ATV children's drama series called *A Bunch of Fives*. ATV was owned by the great impresario Sir Lew Grade, a wonderful man who must be turning in his grave at what's become of TV today. Sir Lew brought all the world's great actors and entertainers – from Olivier to Sammy Davis Jr – to star in high-class dramas and variety shows.

A Bunch of Fives centred around a group of school kids who start up a magazine with the help of one of their teachers, an idea that *Grange Hill* later emulated – plagiarists! The series was directed by an amazing man called John Sichel. John could be very unpredictable. One day he'd be a joy to work with, but the next he'd be a tyrant. He'd shout and make me do things over and over, and it was hard to take. I wasn't used to being bawled out in front of other people – not since boarding school, anyway – and John and I had some real toe-to-toe disagreements.

I recall one occasion when John had been on my case all day, and I called him out to the corridor. He and I'd had enough – we started shouting and swearing and making a right racket. Lord knows what the other actors thought. Eventually, we calmed down and started to discuss our differences, and it was then I realised John was only pushing me so hard to get the best from me. When I went back into the rehearsal room I nailed everything and John got what he wanted from me. It felt great. And at the end of the day John came up and put his arms around me.

'If I didn't care I wouldn't bother pushing you so hard,' he said. 'All that natural anger in you needs to be channelled, Jamie. When you use it instead of letting it use you, you will become a very good actor.'

After that John and I became good friends, and I learned a hell of a lot from him. We went on to do a second series together and he also cast me in quite a few other projects he directed. A good man.

You were so looked after if you worked at ATV. The studios at Borehamwood were a magical place. I had a star dressing room and my own costume dresser – a lovely gay man who would always bring me a bottle of wine at the end of each recording – and Bob Monkhouse used the same dressing room at weekends when they recorded *Celebrity Squares*. I often bumped into Barbara Windsor when she was there. I'd fill her in on how I was getting on, pick her brains and ask her advice on acting, which she always gave graciously and encouragingly.

At lunchtime the canteen was a gallery of stars. On one table you'd spot British film star Kenneth More taking a break from making *Father Brown*, on another Tom Jones while he was recording one of his music specials. I saw Lord Olivier there, although I never went over to speak to him. I wish I had, so I could have thanked him for giving me my first job and show him that I was still working. *The Muppet Show* was filmed at Borehamwood too, and I would often sit and talk to Frank Oz and his gang. Great guys – really friendly and funny. I used to creep into their studio and watch with amazement at how they put the show together. They all looked like they were having so much fun.

Each episode of *The Muppet Show* featured a major star making a guest appearance, and we'd meet them too. One day, as I entered the main reception area and held the door open for someone behind me, I realised it was Rita Moreno, the Broadway star. What a stunning-looking woman. A real Latino beauty, Rita was in a lot of films, including my favourite musical, *West Side Story*. Rita gave me the sexiest look before thanking me. 'It's my pleasure,' I replied, wondering if there was a chance she was flirting with me. I told myself to get a grip. Then again, I thought, maybe she likes them young...

I bumped into her again at lunch and got the same look. Rita was most probably having a lot of fun toying with me. She could have toyed with me all she wanted, but unfortunately I never had the nerve to approach her.

For LWT I went on to a Saturday-morning programme called *Our Show*, which went out straight after *Tiswas*. It was a primetime slot and my job was to interview the heroes of the day. One week I'd be interviewing Carrie

Fisher about a new film she was in – *Star Wars* (I went to the first press screening and was absolutely blown away. I'd never seen effects like it. I got straight on the phone to my mate Pandy and told him how amazing this new film was. It may seem dated now, but then it was ground-breaking cinema) – and the next I'd be sitting in Dickie Davies's seat and using the *World of Sport* studios for a chat with Terry Venables and Ray Wilkins. I was having a ball with it all.

Then there was another TV series down in Bristol – *King of the Castle* – for Harlech TV. A great cast included Fulton Mackay, the nasty screw in *Porridge*. The series was a truly bizarre fantasy where the main character, who was being bullied by – you guessed it – me, escaped into his imagination. Once there, I became a Samurai warrior and all manner of weird and wonderful things took place. The plot was very complicated, and I don't think any of us actors really knew what was going on, but the viewers loved it.

Before I knew it, I was on the telly twice a week – *A Bunch of Fives* on Wednesdays and *King of the Castle* on Sundays – and I was beginning to achieve a little bit of notoriety and fame. That said, the supposed glory of fame was something I never courted. For me it was always about the work. I didn't want my name splashed in the papers, I wanted to act and entertain and be recognised for nothing more than that. This ethos has stood me in good stead over the years, and here's a warning to young actors from an old sage: doing stories on your life in the papers and having your photo taken is no way to go forward. It's the worst day's work you can ever do.

Since the day paper first met ink, the press have built people up, then shot them down just as fast. Court publicity for its own sake and you'll regret it for the rest of your life. Achieve great things as an actor, on the other hand, keep your counsel, and people will always maintain their interest and respect. When it comes to the press, and to fans, be polite, give your autograph and let your work do the talking.

I'm pleased to say that in those early days, and in all the years I've been acting, whatever the press have said about my father – and my involvement with him – has never closed any doors for me professionally. Not that I'm aware of, anyway. I've never been refused a job because of my background or who I am. If anything, who I am and where I come from helped me in the early days. Back then, people in the industry didn't give two hoots about such trivialities – it was the acting they were interested in, and little else. One man in particular – Paul Knight, who I mentioned briefly before – was always behind me in so many ways. Paul has been responsible for some of the greatest TV ever made in this country, and he often called me up with ideas for my next job. It's down to people like him that I've always had work, and I can't thank him enough.

Although acting was always a joy, none of it had really meant anything to me while Dad had been out of reach. It was only once he came back that I really began to flourish, and one of my proudest moments was the first time my father got to see me doing what I loved on stage. I was nearly 20, focusing on theatre work, and had landed a part in *Gotcha*, an iconic one-hour play by Barrie Keeffe. It's about disaffected youth within a failing education system, and, loving the part, I went for it with gusto. Actors such as Karl Johnson and Phil Davis had been in *Gotcha* and I saw the role as a fantastic opportunity. My TV work had been great, but mainly for kids, and this was the first adult work I really got my teeth into. It was a meaty, weighty part, something that required that little extra passion and commitment.

A brilliant director called Adrian Shergold – who'd acted with me on *A Bunch of Fives* – had suggested me for the part, and before I knew it I was working under Richard Ireson with proper actors in a proper acting environment. The play was put on at the Croydon Warehouse, a well-established and respected lunchtime theatre on the fringe circuit that Adrian and Richard ran together.

My character was 'the Kid', a rebellious teenager who catches two teachers – played by Peter White and Penny Casdagli – at it in a storeroom and holds them hostage for an hour by holding a cigarette over the open petrol cap of a motorbike. A wonderful, demanding part to play. The mind games at work reveal the Kid to be much more intelligent than the teachers previously gave him credit for, and I simply loved the dramatic tension of it all. The audience were so close to the stage that the actors were practically in their laps, and the lack of distance between us and them made for an immediacy and intensity that I thrived on. You could feel the audience were genuinely frightened by the power of this teenager who was only a couple of yards away, and playing him was a real thrill.

The day Dad came along with the rest of the family gave me such a feeling of pride. It meant the world to have him in the audience looking at living proof I was going somewhere. I'd first told Dad of my acting ambitions while he was behind bars, and now the result of that conversation was on stage before him. Amusingly, though, the audience got to see a little bit more than was intended during this performance.

One of the play's scenes involves the PE teacher getting so frustrated that he gives the Kid a good hiding – a savage beating, to be precise – and Peter White and I had practised very hard to make the moment as convincing as possible. Peter is one of our most powerful stage actors, and in the end we worked out the scene so it was just right. During his onslaught I would face away from the audience and lie with my hands cupped against my chest so that Peter could kick into my hands. This made things look and sound pretty realistic, but on this occasion art imitated life a little too much – Peter missed my hands and kicked me right across the jaw!

My head snapped back, my family gasped, and for a second poor Peter froze. He's such a gentle soul, and I could see him trying to hide his horror. I was pretty dazed for a few moments, but the adrenalin of being on stage kept me going. The show had to go on! I looked up at Peter and subtly indicated to him to keep going. He gave me another few kicks, this time squarely into my hands, and soon enough the curtain was down and Peter was off fetching some ice for my sore head.

I knew my parents would be worried, so I rushed out to see them. The pain was really bad now I was offstage, but soon we were all laughing about it. 'I knew it looked too good,' said Dad. 'He really caught you, didn't he?'

I nodded, but luckily I could take a punch. The eternal young man in me likes to think I could still handle such a mishap. Hopefully, the opportunity for me to find out won't arise.

That afternoon was so special, and I think it meant as much to Dad as it did to me. *Gotcha* was a success, and I went on to appear in *Killing Time*, part of the same trilogy. During that run I was also doing Nigel Baldwin's *Irish Eyes and English Tears* at the Royal Court over in Sloane Square, so was performing twice a day – once in the afternoon, once in the evening. It was as demanding as hell, but I loved it. *Irish Eyes* is about a group of Chelsea FC fans, one of whom strikes up a friendship with a tramp, and I worked alongside some great actors for that production – among them Karl Johnson, Alfred Molina, Chris Fairbank (best known as Albert Arthur Moxey in *Auf Wiedersehen, Pet*) and Ian Redford. They were the hotshot actors of the day, and as the youngest person in the company I felt privileged to be working with all of them. Karl Johnson in particular is one of the nuttiest, most eccentric of people, and an absolute joy to watch on stage. I used to drool watching him and the other guys rehearsing, and I learned so much from them. One afternoon they came to see me in *Killing Time*, which was fantastic and touching too.

It was those guys who first suggested I got myself a different agent. I'd been with the Italia Conti agency for years, and they had been amazing. Conti's were great for kids' stuff, but I wasn't a kid any more, and it was time to move on. Eventually I ended up with the wonderful Bill Horne, sadly now passed away. Bill was pushy, but in the nicest possible way. He saw that I was a little wayward, that I'd nicked some great parts, but he also recognised that I was sometimes a little slapdash, a little unambitious, shall we say. I desperately wanted to act but was lacking in the discipline of going out and getting it. I'd done well so far, but Bill reminded me that my luck wouldn't last for ever. I had to keep putting myself out there, and Bill helped me do just that.

One day Bill called me into his office, saying he

wanted to talk. I was worried I'd done something wrong, but it turned out the opposite was true.

'I've got big plans for you,' he said. 'I think you've got a lot to offer and that you can go far in this business. But you really need to learn the ropes. You've got to go and learn your trade, so no more TV for a while.'

I was loving my TV work, so this wasn't exactly music to my ears. Still, I listened on.

'You've got to further immerse yourself in the fringe scene, go out there and do your apprenticeship. You won't get much money for it, but if you do as I say you'll reap the dividends later on. Trust me.'

I trusted Bill's judgement and, looking back, I was right to. These days you see so many young actors coming up on TV soaps, but, once their part is killed off, their careers often go the same way. Who knows, if I'd stayed in TV with theatre on the side, post-soap obscurity might have been my fate. Luckily, I had Bill to guide me, and I'll forever be grateful to him.

Following that conversation, I ended up performing at just about every fringe theatre in London, and it was during that time that I really made my bones and learned what hard work really meant. I did some great plays with some brilliant actors and honed my craft. And all the while I was still there for Dad and the business. All things considered, I was working my socks off, and the combination of theatre and work with Dad meant I had a few quid in my pocket too.

But it wasn't a case of all work and no play making Jack a dull boy. When not hard at it, the chaps knew how to relax, and there was plenty of socialising. Mondays and Thursdays were the firm's two drinking days. Business was often involved, but the point was to have a good drink with the people closest to your heart. The A & R was a regular haunt, and not just Mondays and Thursdays either. Dad and I often dropped by after his morning meets. We'd park up behind Charing Cross Road, walk up Denmark Street – or Tin Pan Alley – and up into Ronnie and Mick's place. You were bang in the centre of London, but once you entered the A & R you were shut off from everything and in another world. All the shoplifters used to come in offering whatever they'd nicked that morning, and more often than not I'd end up buying something nice for myself, Mum or whatever girl I was seeing at the time. Shoplifters were brilliant in those days – you never had to buy anything over the counter, as they had it all covered: cashmere jackets, suits, fine shoes, handbags, jewellery. They were like Savile Row tailors – once they knew your size they never forgot. You'd be having a drink and one of them would approach you. 'You're a 42 short, aren't you, Jamie? I've got a lovely Aquascutum two-piece suit. Look lovely on you. Three hundred, but I'll take a oner for it.' If you wanted something, chances were you'd find it at the A & R.

Dad's bar at the Ellerslie was a good place. A

wonderful environment to drink in. But it was just one of several little 'shush clubs' Dad had set up with Uncle George all round South London. They were unlicensed drinking dens – similar in nature to the American 'speakeasy' – and were always filled with diverse, edgy and characterful crowds intent on keeping their drinking times alive after hours.

Wherever we drank, it felt so natural standing shoulder to shoulder with the chaps. These were my dad's friends and my uncles, and being part of their world gave me a sense of belonging and confidence that I've always been grateful for. Their grace and manners rubbed off on me and have carried me through many a situation in life that I might otherwise have shirked from.

When I wasn't out with Dad, I'd be with my best friends Pandy and John Bunce. John was a fellow South Londoner who had also gone to Conti's, but had left just before I'd arrived. He and Pandy were very close. John's family and mine turned out to have connections. John's dad Joe – a lovely man sadly no longer with us – had a waste-paper business down by Lambeth Walk, where a lot of my family come from. It also emerged that John and I had played football against each other when I was at Christ's College and he was at Riverdale, another private school in South London. I always maintain we beat them, while he maintains they beat us. That aside, John and I are as close as can be. He has been a staunch and loyal friend to me. There is a favour he did for me that I will remain eternally grateful for. But more of that later.

The three of us became inseparable, along with Pandy's brother Nick, who I nicknamed Paz. Our favourite watering hole was a club on the King's Road, Chelsea, called J Arthur's. We lived and died in that place. It was a real hotspot, frequented by a lot of Dad's friends, including the Dennis brothers, Roy and Jerry, John Bindon, Terry De Havilland, the famous shoe designer, and my old friend Roy Nash, so I was always well looked after. And you'd find yourself sitting in the restaurant area next to Elton John and Freddie Mercury. I loved it down there.

I also went drinking with my South London pals – smart guys who were all at it and good money-getters. It was the late seventies, people had a bit more money in their pockets, and South London was once again buzzing with its own hotspots – blinding pubs that were just as my dad's had been ten years before. Anyone from South London will remember the Gladstone, Lymans and the Southwark Park Tavern – all legendary places that played fantastic music. But, when it came to music, Lymans was king. They had all the best 12-inch imports, from disco to funk to jazz. We'd drink to the sound of Donna Summer, Earth, Wind & Fire, Change, George Benson and McFadden & Whitehead. 'Ain't No Stopping Us Now' was a favourite, and in many ways the song sums up how I felt in those heady days.

And then there were the other clubs I frequented. In those days you really could get a drink in London 24 hours a day. On any particular night I might go from one club in Mayfair – often Legends – to another in Soho, to the old Embassy off Piccadilly, to Tramp in Jermyn Street, then end up in Reilly's club near Pentonville Prison in the Caledonian Road, or a drinker that Alfie Gerrard, Dad's best friend, had in Islington.

Sunday was always a lovely day. All the chaps and their families would congregate at the Grange, a lovely little boozer run by my auntie Mary and uncle Tom. We'd listen to Sinatra, Jolson and all the jazz standards before having a sing-song until the roast potatoes were ready. Just like we did, they also used to make them extra salty so you'd drink more, and it made for a wonderful atmosphere. Everyone would head over to the Ringside, a restaurant in Old Street owned by former British boxing champion Vic Andretti. Vic's place did an unbeatable Sunday lunch. Sundays were a true day off: everybody was relaxed and life couldn't have been better.

Throughout those electrifying times, girls were always flitting in and out of my life, and I had many, many dalliances, but I was never serious about anyone in particular. Always very wary of committing, I preferred to keep my options open, and I suppose I was a bit of a player for a while. But all of that changed one day when I was having a drink in the Southwark Park Tavern.

I happened to glance up as the door opened, and in walked the most beautiful creature I'd ever seen. A cross between Ursula Andress, Bo Derek and Christie Brinkley, she was perfection on legs, a South London girl who looked like she was from California. 'She' turned out to be 17-year-old Julie Dennis, one of London's hottest models, who featured in the biggest ads of the day. Back then, Julie's face was everywhere – billboards, magazine and telly commercials – and she was making a great name for herself. My jaw dropped to my chest. In that moment I knew I was looking at the woman I had to be with. As anyone in love knows, when you know, *you know*, and boy did I know.

But there was just one problem. While I was footloose and fancy free, Julie was in a relationship. Worse still, her boyfriend turned out to be one of my mates, and there was no way I was going to go stepping on anyone's toes.

Oh well, I thought, good things come to those who wait. I'll catch up with her one of these days. So I decided to bide my time.

Well, I did quite a bit of biding, but it was worth it. Eventually, Julie split from the fellow and I had my chance. Having known each other for quite a while, we had become good *friends*. But now I could let her know how I really felt and so I asked her out. Luckily, she felt the same and said yes. My heart soared. I'll never forget our first date. Julie wore a sky-blue parachute-silk jumpsuit. It had zips everywhere, including a long one down the front, which she wore provocatively low. I spent the whole bloody night trying desperately not to get caught staring at her wonderful cleavage. I still tremble at the memory.

With her beautiful blonde hair and blue eyes, she looked *breathtaking*. I took her to Legends and we danced to Johnny Mathis's 'Gone, Gone, Gone'. It felt like the start of a beautiful relationship.

How life had changed. I had Dad, I had money, I had family. I was thriving in a world of contrasts and I was in love. Everything was rosy, and for the first time in years I felt truly happy and at ease.

10

THE PACKAGE

I wasn't sure what, but I could tell Dad was putting
something together. There was no question something
big was going down. I could feel it.

My first inkling came on a family holiday to Cyprus.
After a few days of relaxing, Dad announced he was
slipping off to India. He didn't say why he was going, and
we all knew better than to ask. Dad's business was his
business, and we were too busy enjoying the delights of
Cyprus to worry about prying. A few days later, Dad was
back on the island, and laden with some of the most
beautiful silk shirts I'd ever seen. He told us about the
wild beauty of India, and left it there. Naturally, I did
wonder what business had taken him to India, but that

was anyone's guess. I concluded one thing, though: he wasn't there to check out the silk trade.

When we got back to London, it was business as usual. Almost, anyway. I was still driving Dad everywhere, but even more often than before – he'd managed to lose his licence and I'd managed to pass my test, so he needed me more than ever. This suited me fine, as there was nothing I wouldn't do to help him.

We kept on doing the familiar rounds, the various meets, but there was a subtle difference in the way Dad went about his business. In the past he had never been complacent about his security – we'd always kept an eye out for anyone on our tail, and our noses on alert for danger – but now Dad was suddenly being extra vigilant about covering his tracks. There was a seriousness about him that told me something big was being planned, and he soon trained me up to be even more careful as I moved around.

Instead of dropping Dad at a meet and waiting for him outside, I'd be told to drive off and meet him elsewhere, sometimes the other side of town. We stopped turning up to meets at someone's front door, but would pull up round the block and walk down a few alleyways and enter via the back garden. We'd swap cars regularly, often once or twice a day, and walk into Underground stations only to emerge minutes later on the other side of the street. I asked no questions, but still lapped up every minute of those surreptitious days.

One thing I knew was Dad wasn't being paranoid. It was Mum who noticed that, as Dad and I left the house each morning, two suspicious-looking guys – obviously cops – would emerge from the house opposite and jump into a car. We were being followed all right, and accordingly I became a master of the U-turn. At first, Dad would tell me when to turn, but soon enough I developed an intuition for when was the right time. There we'd be, driving along in silence, eyes in the rear-view, and I'd spin round at just the right moment, put my foot down and pull over at a nearby café. We'd have a cup of tea, keep a lookout and only move once sure the coast was clear.

All the subterfuge didn't faze me one bit. This was pure, unadulterated excitement. The way we moved around reminded me of the word 'tradecraft', often found in the novels of John le Carré or Len Deighton, referring to espionage techniques. Sure, I wasn't a cold-war spy, but the myriad ways I covered my tracks sure as hell made me feel like one. There was an undeniable romance and drama to those days that the actor in me grew addicted to. Not being able to tell anyone about it, and the mystery of why we were creeping about, only added to the thrill of it all.

A lot of plotting and planning went on, and there was one man in particular Dad and I began to spend a lot of time with – Colin 'Duke' Osbourne. As I later discovered, it was thanks to Duke that Dad became involved in the mysterious adventure I was on the periphery of. Dad and Dukey went way back to the 1960s. Over the years, Duke had established himself as a fine armed robber – a real money-getter – and in the East End he was known as the man who looked after the Krays' arsenal. But Dad had lost touch with him, and it was chance that brought them back together.

Dad got wind of a man who was frequenting one of his little spielers on the Old Kent Road and regularly losing a fortune. The bloke had gained such a reputation for losing that punters were literally queuing up to beat him. He was giving away untold fortunes, so Dad became intrigued to find out who it was. Lo and behold, it was Duke.

Duke was a true character. Very tall and lanky, in his mid-forties with long hair, he dressed impeccably – a sort of gentrified hippy look – and lived in a beautiful penthouse apartment in Sutton. We used to call him 'Pasha' as he was like a Turkish prince, always playing host to a harem of young people who gathered at his home to while away the time and listen to Duke's stories of underworld adventure. Duke was a true raconteur, forever drinking vast quantities of strong tea and never tiring of company. He was a flirtatious man, who had a penchant for young men, but once we'd established I wasn't that way inclined we became great friends.

It soon became clear where Duke was getting his money from: cannabis. He'd moved into supplying it in a big way, and that meant hefty paydays. Like so many armed robbers at the time, Duke had stopped going out on the pavement in favour of supplying 'puff' to a booming market. Times had changed for armed robbers – Dukey had done seven years for a past robbery, but knew full well that getting done for a similar offence in the late seventies meant a sentence three or four times as harsh. It just wasn't worth it any more, and a lot of the criminal fraternity felt the same way. There was a lot of money to be had dealing marijuana, and the risks were comparatively tiny – a 20-month sentence versus 20 years. A no-brainer. Added to that, no one was getting hurt. The dope trade was pretty peaceful back then, and being able to leave weapons out of it made everyone involved feel a lot safer.

As for demand, people couldn't get enough of the stuff. Everyone I knew liked a puff, and in those days marijuana wasn't adulterated with other substances like it is today. There was no 'skunk', and everyone considered dope a take-it-or-leave-it kind of drug. Half the pub owners we knew were happy if people were having a sly smoke, as it meant there'd be no trouble – I've got many happy memories of watching roomfuls of people chilling out, dancing and laughing all night without one bit of trouble kicking off.

I'd been introduced to puffing while hanging out with Dad and his friends. 'You like a cigarette, don't you, Jamie?' someone had said, passing me a joint. 'Well, have a puff on that.' Some people would be up in arms about a father condoning his son using drugs, but I know that Dad was happy for me to try it because he always preferred having things out in the open, and would far rather have me smoke around him than be off behind his back and potentially getting in too deep. Just as Dad first had a drink with me, and taught me how to act responsibly with it, I had my first smoke with him and learned there's no harm in it if you take it easy.

I feel the same way about my kids – I believe that taking the mystery out of something is the only way to stop people running amok and getting themselves into trouble. It's all about education, and I think children tend to respond well if you give them boundaries – it's the unknown that can send them down the wrong path. These days it's inevitable a teenager is going to encounter marijuana somewhere along the line, and I'd much rather tell my kids what's what than have them meeting some lowlife in a pub who only wants to get them hooked on other substances down the line.

There was some amazing gear going around back in the seventies. One week it would be Thai sticks – beautiful buds wrapped around sticks like toffee apples – some of the best puff ever. You'd laugh all night on it without a trace of anxiety or paranoia. Then there was Red Lebanese, another marvellous variety. But the crème de la crème was Red Seal Afghanistan Black, smuggled from the Afghan mountains through Nepal and Pakistan straight through to London. It was black, like rubber, in kilo slabs, and I'll never forget the way it used to break off in your hands.

Dukey was a major supplier, that much I knew, but I had no idea what he and Dad had planned. I didn't see that it was my place to ask, although I was starting to suspect it was drugs, and that it was big. It turned out I was right. I was never given precise details, but I gathered this much: there was a parcel on its way. It was coming from overseas, and inside was a ton and a half of Afghanistan Black. Dukey had organised the route and Dad had agreed to help him shift it.

I was staggered. Forget kilo slabs, this was over two million quid's worth – that's 20 million in today's money. *Now* I understood what all the months of planning and subterfuge had been about – a good few heads would have been put together to shift something that massive across continents. It would have been necessary to find all sorts of trustworthy people, to try out the smuggling route over and over, to make the plan watertight.

One and a half tons, that's all I knew. It was exciting, audacious, scary, and the more meets we went on, the more new faces I encountered. Things were hotting up, the date was drawing near. But there was a problem.

A source informed Dad that Customs had been sniffing around a major drugs-smuggling operation for months. Was it Dukey's? Would Dad be implicated? There was no way of telling.

Could Dad have pulled out? No.

Why? The drugs had passed through too many hands around the world. People could not be let down.

The ball was already rolling.

The package was in transit.

It was on.

Danger has always lived with my dad. The possibility of being watched never put Freddie Foreman off – on the contrary, Dad always saw difficult situations as challenges to be overcome. Running scared was to admit defeat. In his mind, half the fun was negotiating himself out of tricky situations. Part of the buzz of what he did, I imagine.

If Dad was worried the police were on to him, he kept it to himself, but in hindsight I can see that he must have been feeling the heat, because a couple of weeks before the consignment was due to arrive I found that my services were no longer required. No longer did he ask me to drive him around, and suddenly there were no more errands to run. In short, my father was protecting me. If anything bad was going to happen, he wanted me out of harm's way. Typical Fred, always looking out for his own, always putting others first.

Accordingly, I was in the dark. I stayed busy with acting work, and all I could do was keep my counsel and wait. If that was what my father needed me to do, it was fine by me.

THE PACKAGE

One night late in 1978 – around October – Dukey turned up at the front door. A little unusual: we normally saw him at his place. Stranger still, he was staying the night. He'd never done that before. Strange, yes, but nevertheless we all had a lovely evening – Mum made dinner and we all talked and laughed as usual. Nothing was amiss. I asked no questions, got told no lies, and went to bed.

When I awoke the next morning, Dad and Duke had disappeared, and I was still none the wiser.

They had left at the crack of dawn, and driven through early-morning London. Months of planning and coordination had led to this moment. Scores of people around the world had done their bit, and now it was time for Dad to do his.

The plan was crystal clear in their minds as they sped through empty streets. The two men drove with steely, silent intent, put Dad's car in a lock-up and switched to a bent Ford Zephyr. In the boot was a selection of cutting gear strong enough to tear through metal. And of course a set of scales – no prizes for guessing what they were for.

Their destination: a long-distance-lorry depot in Aldgate in the East End. Awaiting them was an empty lorry. Empty-looking, at least. Hidden in the walls and floor of the 42-foot container was 1.5 tons of the finest cannabis in the world. All Dad and Duke had to do was cut it out and weigh it. But first the lorry had to be moved.

Cautiously, they approached the depot and met with the lorry driver, Eddie Watkins, or 'Scatty Eddie'. It was time to get going.

Dad and Duke drove ahead in the Zephyr to make sure the roads were clear. A few miles on and it all looked good. No roadblocks, no suspicious cars – apart from an old man and a woman sitting silently in a parked vehicle by the motorway. The sight of them worried Dad a little, but he gave it the benefit of the doubt. Dad eased up on the accelerator until Eddie caught up and overtook – now Dad could mind the lorry from behind and make sure it wasn't being tailed.

All was still quiet on the road, and before long the lorry slipped off the motorway and rolled into its destination, a well-concealed wrecked car yard in the middle of nowhere. It was time to get cutting and get out. Nearly. One last check was needed. Before they began, Dad asked the yard owner's son-in-law to ride his motorbike around the surrounding lanes to make sure they were alone.

They weren't.

Somehow Customs officers were on to them. They were a mile or so away, waiting patiently to trap the men when they drove out with a car full of gear. Terrible news, and proof enough that the message Dad had received about Customs indeed applied to Dad and Dukey. They knew it was on them, and their hearts began to sink. All those months for this.

It was time for plan B. The lorry had to be moved, but retracing the route back down the lane to the motorway was out of the question. Luckily, Dad had already worked out an alternative: the lorry would drive through a farmer's field and cut back on to tarmac that way.

Dad instructed Eddie where to go, and told him to head for the coffee stall by the lorry stop at Blackheath.

The Zephyr was first to arrive at the heath. Dad and Dukey got out of the car and sat on the grass. Sensing the cops would be taking photos, Dad pulled his duffel coat over his head and waited for Eddie to show up. Minutes later, the lorry rumbled up the hill and shuddered to a stop. Eddie jumped down from the cab, and made his way towards the men, but nobody acknowledged each other. Eddie positioned himself within earshot, and stared ahead as if they were strangers. When you're sitting on a couple of millions' worth of gear and Customs are your audience, acting familiar with each other isn't clever.

The game was up. There was nothing for it but to try to escape. The package had to be abandoned, but Dad knew that the police could only store such a large lorry in the depot – the idea that he might be able to break in later on offered some consolation. That aside, he needed to think on his feet if they were to have any hope of getting out of this. In a few minutes, he hatched another plan.

'We need to leave the gear,' he told Eddie. 'If they can't nick you with the puff, they haven't got anything on you, so follow me and Duke. We'll drive ahead, go through the Blackwall Tunnel and stop at the other end. The cops'll be on you, so, before you get out of the tunnel, jack-knife the lorry, block 'em in, and run to the end. We'll be waiting for you.'

Eddie nodded. The men stood up, and went back to their vehicles. As Eddie fired his engine up, several other ignition keys must have turned simultaneously. The Customs officers were waiting for the perfect moment to pounce.

Dad and Dukey slipped away as planned, headed for the tunnel, sped through and pulled up on the other side. Eddie waited a while and followed, but, for reasons that will always remain a mystery, Scatty Eddie didn't do as he was told. Rather than jack-knifing the lorry in the tunnel and making a run for it, he simply kept on trucking right out the southern end. Dad and Duke looked on wide-eyed as the lorry steamed past them, closely followed by a procession of cars packed with Customs men.

It was all over for Eddie. Nobody could help him now. Doubtless he'd pull over somewhere, give himself up and get nicked. Dad and Duke had no idea why Eddie hadn't stuck to the plan, but they had better things to worry about. Everything was fucked up, and now they had to make themselves scarce. The men parted company and went straight into hiding. Eddie had a prison stretch – maybe a five or a seven – coming his way, but Dad and Duke were damned if they were going to join him.

Dad didn't head home to get nicked, but made his way over to 'bacon sandwiches' to work out his next move. As he sipped his tea and dug into one of Nan's trademark doorsteps, he wondered, if there was a chance he could still nick the gear from the depot. There was a lot of other people's money at stake here, after all, and getting the gear back would avoid a whole lot of grief. He soon got his answer when he switched on the telly.

As the news headlines rolled, Dad stared in total disbelief. Something truly terrible had happened. A Customs officer had been shot in Aldgate.

It turned out that, once out of the tunnel, Eddie had driven back to Aldgate, parked in the lorry depot, locked the lorry and started to walk away. The Customs officers chose this as their moment to pounce, but, instead of holding his hands up and doing an 'I'm just the driver' act, Eddie pulled out a Beretta pistol and shot the poor Customs guy dead. In a split second the stupid bastard went from being a driver to a murderer, and an innocent man with a family had been killed for doing his job. Total fucking madness. What on earth went through Eddie's mind is anyone's guess, but he certainly lived up to his nickname. It was a tragedy on so many levels.

Dad was absolutely horrified. It was all totally unnecessary. What's more, from day one Dad had insisted that no guns should be involved – he had no idea about Eddie's hidden shooter. When Dad was at work his *modus operandi* was to make sure no 'straight goers' ever got hurt. Killing innocents was completely beyond the pale. So much for Eddie's five or seven: now he would be looking at life. As for Dad and Duke, now they would be wanted for both smuggling and accessory to murder, and all because of one man's stupidity. It was a total fucking disaster.

All the while, I'd been going about my day blissfully unaware of what Dad and Duke had been up to, never mind what had gone down with Eddie. I even glimpsed a newsflash about the dead Customs man, but didn't put two and two together – whatever the plans for retrieving the stash, I knew guns would be a million miles away.

I only felt a bit of an alert when a message arrived telling me to get over to Auntie Nanette's. Christ! I thought, and prayed none of what I'd seen on TV was linked to my father. It was impossible, I told myself as I jumped in the car and sped to be by his side.

As I've said, Dad is a master of the poker face, a consummate professional at keeping cool when the heat is on, but Eddie's actions had pushed Freddie Foreman's self-control to breaking point. I walked into Auntie Nanette's, and Dad was absolutely livid as he recounted the day's terrible events to me. Dad hadn't condoned Eddie's behaviour on any level, and now Eddie had implicated my father in something *very* heavy.

Listening, I was completely flabbergasted. A thousand

bove left: My dad with the lovely Barbara Windsor, who gave me sound advice when
·was starting out in acting.

bove right: My amazing Mumsy, Maureen, who is always there for me through thick
·nd thin.

·elow and overleaf, above: As Bill Sykes in Roman Polanski's film of *Oliver Twist*, both
·n and off camera. When I was a kid, there were pictures of Dickens characters on the
·alls of my dad's pub so to grow up and play one of the most iconic was a real honour.

Below: With Ross Kemp in hit TV series *Without Motive*.

Julie modelling when she was 18 years old. You can see why I fell for her – she's as
autiful now as she was then.

Above: I love Julie as much today as I did when I first saw her: she is the love of my life.

Right: Julie and her adorable mum, Pat.

Above: Me with my stepson, Billy and my son, Alfie.

Below: With (left to right) Roy Hilder, my mate Pandy and my dad.

Julie and I were destined to be together; we found each other again after twenty years apart.

My dad.

Some of my later film roles.

Above: Ironically playing a mouthy wannabe gangster 'The Duke' alongside Daniel Craig and Colm Meany in *Layer Cake*.　© *Sony Pictures/The Kobal Collection/Smith, Dan*

Below: As Mark in Gary Oldman's hard-hitting masterpiece *Nil By Mouth*.

© *SE8 Group Ltd/Luc Besson/The Kobal Collection/English, J* thoughts shot through my mind. Aside from my shock at Eddie's actions, and my sadness for the Customs officer, I felt frightened as I considered the possible ramifications of this nightmare. I'd only had Dad back a couple of years, and now this. Dad's angry reaction said it all: everything was so fucked up, and we both knew he was in serious danger.

We had to work out what to do next, and quick. The police would already be scouring London for Dad, and probably me too. Dad was sure they would know I had no involvement in what had gone down. But they'd observed me driving him around for months, and at the very least would want yours truly to answer a few questions. Dad needed to go underground, but both of us gone AWOL would look like an admission of guilt on my part. It was decided that I would carry on as normal while Dad stayed in hiding.

I left Nan's, and shot around town passing on various messages to chaps who needed to know what had happened. The old machine went to work again, this time to make sure Dad was squirreled away safe and sound, and everybody needed to have their stories straight in case the Old Bill came calling.

I'd be lying if I said I wasn't deeply, deeply concerned about what had happened – all the memories of previous trials, of life without my father during the prison years, hovered around the edge of my consciousness, but I had to be strong, get my head together and focus on the moment. Stay calm, Jamie, I thought. Keep cool and there might be a way out of this. Let yourself dwell, and there might be a repeat performance. Deal with the chaps. Let the network take care of Dad. Carry on as normal.

It was a Friday night, and acting normal meant going out for a drink. Knowing the police would be watching me like hawks, I met up with a few mates and acted as if nothing was amiss. I dropped into a few clubs, then went to see an uncle and passed on a message from Dad. After that it was home to bed. I sat tight on Saturday with Mum, making sure she was all right, all the while hoping Dad was OK and conscious of the police glaring at the house. We waited for the inevitable knock on the door, but bedtime came and we hadn't heard a peep.

Sunday, day of rest. Not for the cops, though, and on this occasion not for me. No sooner had I opened my eyes than I was staring up the barrels of a .45 and a .38, both pointed straight at my head. Holding them were two officers, one from Customs and one from the Flying Squad. Bloody hell, I thought, this is a bit much.

'Get up, Jamie,' said the Customs officer. 'We need to talk.'

Over the years one thing I'd learned from Dad was this: when a policeman is pointing a gun at you, he's always nervous, often more nervous than you are. And nerves and guns aren't a good combination – it only takes the smallest slip of the finger for a pistol to go off.

Dad had had many a police gun pulled on him in the past, and he'd always warned me that, should it ever happen to me, I should do everything I could to keep the situation calm. 'Don't move quickly,' he said, 'and always try to talk them down. Keep the situation as calm as possible. They may be police, but it's not very often they have to handle guns. Accidents happen easily.'

Considering that the officers standing over me had lost one of their own men in the last 48 hours, I knew they'd be pretty upset. They certainly looked edgy enough – you could see their hands trembling as they pointed their guns at me. In a split second I remembered Dad's advice.

'OK, relax,' I said, not moving a muscle. 'Just let me get dressed and I'll put the kettle on.'

The pair of them eased off a little, and I gave them a nod to let them know I wasn't going to try to do anything clever. 'There's no need for them,' I added, looking at the guns. 'My mum and sister are in the house. I don't want any trouble. Really.'

We went downstairs. I made some tea while the police turned the house over. I knew they wouldn't find anything, so I relaxed as I poured the milk into the cups. Meanwhile, I could hear Mum going to work with the police.

'What are you doing coming in here with your guns drawn while my little girl's in bed? Don't you know I'm under the doctor at the moment with heart trouble? Frightening the life out of us – who do you think you are?'

Good old Mum. Obviously she was in bits about what had happened with Dad, but she wasn't going to let the cops see that. I've seen her kick into gear a few times, and when it comes to putting on a brave face – and some fantastic acting to boot! – she's as solid as a rock. A truly formidable woman.

'Where's Fred?' asked the officers.

'Your guess is as good as mine,' she said, hamming up the dramatics. 'We had a row so he's probably still out on the booze. What do I care anyway? I hope he never comes back.'

Now it was my turn.

'What's this all about?' I asked, walking in with the tea. 'What do you want to talk to my dad about?'

The cops never give anything away, so I had to take no reply for an answer.

'There's a premises in Marshalsea Road with your dad's name on the lease,' said the copper. 'We want to take a look, Jamie.'

If their detective minds seriously thought Dad would be hiding out in his own property, I was more than happy to waste a bit of their time showing them around. 'No problem, officer, I'll just get my keys.'

The premises was a four-storey building, a former doss-house Dad had converted. There was a boxing club on one floor, a photographer's studio on another, and a gymnasium. The basement was Dad's office and a rehearsal studio that my brother Gregory ran. Many of the best gigging bands in London rehearsed there, including Paul Young's group. But, as it was 9am on a Sunday, I knew the place would be deserted when me and five carloads of armed officers showed up.

These police do like their guns, I thought, as, weapons drawn, a little army of officers surrounded the empty building – I hoped it was empty anyway. I knew Dad was elsewhere, but for a second it crossed my mind that I didn't know where Dukey had disappeared to.

What followed was serious and scary, but also pretty farcical. Guns drawn, countless cops followed me into the building, only to be met by … nothing. I took them down to the rehearsal room, and I'll never forget the sight of two cops approaching our little upright piano, pointing their guns at it, and gingerly lifting the lid.

'For fuck's sake,' I laughed, 'I couldn't fit in there, never mind my dad.'

The cops looked up a little sheepish; I think they saw my point. We moved to the back of the building, and arrived at a locked door. It only led to a stairwell, but we always kept it locked because several people – Dad included – had said they had seen a ghost and felt a strange presence there. No matter the weather, that stairwell was always freezing cold, and it gave us all the heebee-jeebies. The police told me to open it up and, truthfully, I said I didn't have a key and that it only led to a stairwell.

That wasn't good enough for them. There was a hinged pane of glass above the door, and a few coppers were giving it the eye. 'I'll go through it, Guv,' said one, and what followed was pure slapstick.

Using a ladder, the copper climbed up to the window. I waited till he'd clambered halfway through it before piping up with an interesting little anecdote.

'We keep the door locked because the building is haunted,' I said casually. 'Through there's where the ghost lives.'

The poor guy froze as I spoke, his legs dangling from the window, and the men burst into laughter as their fellow officer struggled not to bottle out. 'You're not going to take any notice of that old twaddle, are you?' shouted someone as the cop dropped through the window. There was a key on the other side and, quick as a flash, the bloke unlocked the door and jumped through it. He was white as a sheet.

Peals of laughter. Thank God, I thought, at least things are a bit more relaxed now. Still, none of the coppers exactly rushed forward. 'You go first,' said one. 'No you,' said another. One minute they'd been running around toting guns like they were in *The Sweeney* and the next they're seemingly reluctant to go down the stairs because of a ghost. If anything, those moments with the cops offered a little bit of light relief from the tension of a terrible situation.

Satisfied there was nobody in the building but a ghost, the cops vacated it. Outside, I had a word with a few officers from the Flying Squad.

'What's going on? What's this all about?' I asked guardedly.

They told me the story. The plot to infiltrate Dukey's drug run had been going for 18 months, and was called Operation Wrecker, so named by Customs and Excise in reference to smuggling a few centuries back, when teams of 'wreckers' used to direct ships carrying valuables on to perilous rocks along the Cornish coast. Once the ships had washed up, goods were stolen and sold on. A wholly different form of smuggling from a bygone era.

Customs had worked alongside the police, and observed the lorry going to and from Pakistan for 18 months. Dukey's crew had brought in some £10 million, but, when it came to the swoop at Aldgate, Customs wanted to take the lorry alone. Maybe they wanted all the glory – who knows? – but I got the impression the police felt the confrontation could have been handled differently if they had been involved.

When Eddie left the lorry that fateful morning, the Customs officers had steamed in tooled up to the eyeballs, and, though there's no excusing what Scatty Eddie did, perhaps a less aggressive approach could have saved a man's life. Perhaps a police presence would have kept the situation under control. There's never much point in what-might-have-beens, but all I know is that a man lost his life that day for no good reason, and Scatty Eddie went on to serve 25 years at Her Majesty's pleasure before dying in prison. Two wasted lives, and for what?

Hearing about Operation Wrecker made me angry and sad – Dad was only involved with a small part of the operation for a very short time, but his brief association would be enough to land him in big trouble. I already knew he would have to keep his head down for a very long time. As I said goodbye to the officers, I began to wonder what on earth was going to happen next.

'When your Dad turns up, tell him to come in and see us,' said one of the Flying Squad coppers.

'If I see him, I'll let him know,' I said, 'but these rows with Mum happen all the time.'

I left it there.

11

ON THE RUN

Apart from Dad, none of his firm had been involved with Dukey, but, immediately the chaps found out the shit had hit the fan, they rallied around and made sure he was safe. A house was located and within hours Dad was safely ensconced in a North London estate.

My father was out of sight, but not out of mind, and he needed someone to run messages for him. I couldn't have let anyone but me do that job. I was desperate to know Dad was OK, and prepared to do anything to make sure of it. From then on in, I was the go-between for Dad and the chaps. Looking back, perhaps it didn't make that much sense for the son of a man being actively sought by the police to be running errands to and from a hideout – they had their eye on me, after all – but I felt compelled to take that mantle for the sake of my father and my family. And anyway I was sure I could outwit the cops with a bit of good old-fashioned tradecraft.

I only moved at night. One of my TV mates lived in Battersea and owned a VW Camper, so en route to Dad I'd make a few detours and wind up at Richard's place in Prince of Wales Drive. I'd walk in the front entrance, duck out the back door, jump in his van and speed off to see Dad. Richard never asked any questions, so I didn't have to tell him any lies. Coming back, I'd repeat the process backwards. It worked like a charm. Lovely.

Visiting Dad was always wonderful. I'd take him the goodies he wanted, pass some messages on and slip him some money, and in those trying times our moments together were sweet relief. We'd become so accustomed to each other's company on our daily rounds that it was painful being apart, especially for Dad. Being holed up on your own 24/7 is hard enough for anyone, but add to that the fear of the unknown and you've got a situation fit to make you crack. Dad stayed strong, but I know his spirits were low.

At some point it became necessary for Dad to switch safe houses, and the chaps found him another place to keep his head down. His new residence was above a nightclub in Tottenham, but not until my first visit did I realise his room overlooked the yard of the local police station. Talk about keeping your enemies close. I couldn't believe it.

'How can you live here?' I asked him, incredulous.

'Well, if you're going to hide, where better than right under their bloody noses?' laughed Dad.

He had a point, and the view of the coppers coming and going was an amusing distraction. Still, it did end up a bit stressful in the end, and Dad soon moved on again.

The story was all over the papers. Duke's face appeared on the front page of the *Sun* as the most wanted man in Britain, and the police were scrambling to locate him. Faces from Duke's end were being nicked left, right and centre, and the disgusting thing was some of these so-called friends were spilling their guts to the authorities, making statements against poor old Dukey to save their own skins.

I relayed messages between Dad and Duke, and with a murder charge looming over them it was soon decided they would have to go on their toes and get out of the country. In Dad's world, you can't hide in London forever. There was nothing else for it. I liaised with a contact and after several meetings in various London parks, our man delivered what was needed: fake passports.

I'll never forget the moment I received those passports. I'm no expert but to me they looked bang on the money – beautiful handiwork that you wouldn't give a second glance to. Dukey's photo was fantastic. Gone were his long hippy locks and beard: Pasha had smartened up his act and now looked like a most respectable City gent, nothing like the mug shot in the *Sun*. Dad's was equally impressive. Unlike Duke, Dad was always immaculately groomed, but since bolting to North London he had grown a beard and turned into a bit of a pasha himself. And he had a new name, of course. George Newbury – Godfather of British Anonymity.

Passports in hand, the men were all set to go. But then tragedy struck out of the blue. Ever since disappearing, Dukey had been complaining to the fellow who was minding him of various illnesses and ailments. He requested various medication be brought to him every day. Dukey knew his drugs, and his mate (who didn't) obligingly brought him whatever he required. Little did anyone know, Dukey was faking his symptoms.

Rather than taking the medication, poor Pasha was stockpiling it. Duke had done a 12 stretch in prison before, and had often said he'd rather die than go back. Given his current situation – and despite the passport to help him get away – he couldn't deal with the idea of being on the run, or going back to jail. Dukey was always a man of his word, and his final actions proved how serious he was about never doing any more bird. On 1 December 1979, dear Pasha bathed, shaved, put his best suit on, and took his own life with a lethal cocktail of drugs. On discovering Pasha's body, the man who had been looking after him took him to Hackney Marshes and carefully laid him on the centre spot of a football pitch. Early one foggy morning, Dukey's body was found by a man walking his dog.

We were absolutely devastated at the passing of a great friend and a wonderful character. Pasha was as eccentric, idiosyncratic and kind as they come. He had his reasons for doing what he did, but I think what really pushed him over the edge was the scum who grassed on him. It broke Pasha's heart that people close to him had turned. They know who they are.

Further testament to Pasha's good nature was a note he left with me, which I passed on to a solicitor. In it, he took responsibility for the entire operation: the planning, the smuggling and the financing. Dukey covered the letter with his fingerprints, leaving no doubt about its authenticity. It was so touching that a man about to do away with himself took the time to try to protect my father from harm. Pasha was a true gent.

Kind as it was, Dad knew the letter wouldn't be of much use in a court of law. As always, the powers that be were itching to bring Dad down. One of theirs had been killed, and the police wanted as many heads to roll as possible. With Duke out of the way, Dad was now the main target. All eyes were on my dad, or on his absence, I should say.

Within days the chaps arranged for Dad's exile to Tenerife. The fake passport worked a dream, and I let out a deep sigh of relief when word arrived that he'd got there safely. Mum and Danielle discreetly followed shortly after – they had no reason to hang about, and couldn't face having the Old Bill knocking on the door constantly. By a circuitous route they made their way there.

And then there was one: me.

My situation was complicated, very much a case of 'should I stay or should I go?' On the one hand, the police hadn't pulled me in – not yet anyway – but I knew that, as time went by and they became more frustrated in their efforts to locate Dad, attention would become more focused on me. Would they nick me in an effort to flush Dad out? Would I become a sprat to catch a mackerel? I couldn't say, but it worried me. On the other hand, I was falling deeply in love with Julie and my career looked like it was about to really take off.

My agent Bill's prophecy that good things were going to happen to me seemed about to come true. Thanks to him, I'd laid down a couple of screen tests for a new movie that was soon to be made. As a result I was offered a role in *Quest for Fire*, a film by French director Jean-Jacques Arnaud. It would be a stunning portrayal of early humans' struggle to control fire, and I'd be playing a Neanderthal-like tribesman. A wonderful opportunity. I would be filming on location in the Congo, in deepest Africa. I would also be working alongside some big names – Everett McGill, Ron Perlman, Nameer El-Kadi and the gorgeous Rae Dawn Chong – but the timing couldn't have been worse.

Much as I loved my career, if push came to shove, I was prepared to drop anything and everything for my family. That was never a dilemma, and the same is true to this day. Still, I was in limbo for a few weeks once Dad had gone. Were the police after me or not? Luckily I found out just in time.

I was steering clear of our empty house in Dulwich, only dropping by once a week to check on it. In the meantime, our wonderful neighbours, the Ellisons, were taking in our post for us. One day the police had turned up looking for me while Mr Ellison was picking up the post. Noticing a letter addressed to me, a copper grabbed it and tore it up. He had recognised the DVLA envelope: it contained my driving licence – since passing my test I'd been waiting for it to come through.

'He won't be needing that any more,' said the copper as the remains of my licence landed on our driveway and blew away in the breeze.

That moment said it all. I wasn't safe, and as long as I was around the same went for Dad.

The police had been biding their time, looking for my father, but it was plain I'd soon be hauled in. Who knows what they might have had – photos of me on meets, helping Dad, or tapped phone calls perhaps? It didn't matter. They had finally decided to nick me in an attempt to flush out my dad. If arrested I would most certainly be charged with conspiracy, which would help them build a stronger case against my dad.

I was a wanted man. It was time for me to go on the run.

I received a message to go and see the chaps. They'd organised Dad's departure; now it was my turn to be looked after.

'This is what you do,' they began. The last time I'd heard that phrase was when Dad had told me to go and see Barbara Windsor about getting into acting. How times had changed, I thought. 'Hands' was doing the talking. One of Dad's best friends, Hands was his nickname – I cannot use his real name for obvious reasons.

'You go home and pack a bag. Don't take too much, you'll be travelling light. Then you head to Victoria Station tomorrow morning. From there, take the boat train to Paris. When you arrive in Paris, you go to Charles de Gaulle Airport. Don't worry about using your own name. Just book yourself on the first available flight to Madrid. Now, once in Madrid, you can use any name you want, because you will be taking an internal flight, so think one up and get on a plane to Tenerife. When you arrive in Tenerife, you take a taxi to a place called Los Cristianos. Then you phone this number when you get there.'

A piece of paper was thrust into my hand. On it was a number, and that was all. I wasn't allowed to write down the instructions – everything had to remain in my head. I repeated the plan back to them until I had it word-perfect. By the time I was done, I thought it all sounded pretty simple. As always, the chaps had worked everything out down to the smallest detail. But, as I was to discover; nothing would be as easy as it sounded. These things never are.

'One more thing,' added Hands. 'For your safety and your Dad's, don't tell anyone you are going.'

The inevitable had finally happened. A new chapter in my life was about to begin. The chaps had no idea how long we would have to stay out of the way. When I put that question to Hands, he looked at me sympathetically.

'I don't know, kid. But it could be at least a year or so.'

A year, I thought. *Fucking hell.* It seemed a very long time. But it had to be done. If it was this or a possible jail sentence, I'd rather be sitting on a sunny beach than in a cold prison cell. Still, it gave me a lot to think about. How was this going to affect my career? What would my agent say? I had just got going with Bill Horne. I had built some good contacts and now I would have to put everything on hold. I knew I'd done some good work, and hoped that on my return I would be able to pick up where I'd left off. Thinking further, I realised sticking around didn't really make sense for my career: the press would have a field day if I were to be implicated in what had just gone down. No one would touch me, it would be disastrous. It would be best to stay out of the way – 'Time heals all wounds', as they say.

I have always tried to be a positive person. My glass has always been half full. I decided to make the most of my situation. It would certainly be a new experience. I hadn't seen much of the world and living in a new country – and immersing myself in a different culture – would broaden my horizons. The other big disappointment was having to forgo my burgeoning relationship with the beautiful Julie. I thought back to our first date in Legends nightclub. We'd danced to 'Gone Gone Gone' by Johnny Mathis – how prophetic those words had turned out to be. But I consoled myself with one thought: I had waited for her once, so maybe I would win her back one day in the future. Not being able to say goodbye and explain my sudden departure was hard, though. If only I'd known then what I know now. Unfortunately, it turned out I wouldn't meet Julie again for another *20 years* and an awful lot happened to both of us in that time …

I only told one person I was leaving the country: my brother, Gregory. There were a number of belongings I needed to be kept safe – my beloved record collection (I had the originals of every recording Frank Sinatra had made) and a fine collection of antique jewellery I'd acquired over the years. I knew he'd look after them for me, so that at least I would have something to come back to. After saying goodbye to Gregory, I packed my bag before heading out to Legends for the night. Pandy, Johnny Bunce and Pandy's brother Nick met me there, and we had a night as great as any other. I didn't say a word about my impending departure, not because I didn't have faith in them – Pandy and Johnny are staunch men I'd trust with my life – but because they didn't need to know. I didn't want to weigh them down with knowing what I was up to. Asking someone to keep a secret can be unfair, and many times in life I've found that people can let things go without meaning to. Besides, the chaps had told me to keep my lips sealed. Even if a part of me might have been relieved to get things off my chest, there was no way I would break my code of silence.

The night drew to a close and we said goodnight; no doubt a future date for a drink was mentioned. I stood there, surrounded by the mates who were so dear to me, and wondered how long it would be before we said hello again. 'See you later, chaps,' I said. But in my head I was bidding them farewell. For a while at least.

It was late. As always, the West End was teeming with life. The bright lights of the city and all its charms were so familiar and, now I was about to leave, it all felt more alive and vibrant than ever. People jostled in the streets, crowded in and out of buses and cabs, queued for the late-night clubs. Couples kissed, hustlers hustled, groups of revellers laughed, and I walked briskly past. How I loved my London and everything in it. It was a kaleidoscope of colour and contrast, a melting pot of good and bad, and in the morning I would be leaving my beloved city. Foreign shores beckoned. But I would be back one day. I knew it.

I made my way home. It was time to rest. I got into

bed and looked at my suitcase in the corner of the room. Aside from my gear, it was packed with clothes for my father. Dad had travelled light to Tenerife, and the chaps had asked me to take him what he needed. It was my pleasure, of course. I switched out the light and lay there a while, blinking in the dark. I thought of Dad, of Mum, of Danielle. Family. Forget London, forget friends, forget acting – my flesh and blood mattered more than anything in the world, and I thanked my lucky stars they were safe and I would soon be with them.

Filled with trepidation and excitement, I began to drift off to sleep. Here we go again, I thought. My life had always been packed with twists and turns. As horrible as circumstances were for our family, a new adventure was about to begin, and I knew I was up to the challenge.

I woke up early and set off. It's funny, but knowing what I was up to made me feel very conspicuous just walking down the street. I was used to keeping an eye out for the police, but now I felt like I was painted red with a siren on my head. Every second felt like a minute, every queue and hold-up was the end of the world. I was so impatient to get away, and kept thinking it'd be sod's law if the Old Bill managed to spot me on my way through London. I was very self-conscious, and convinced I looked as guilty as hell.

Arriving at Victoria, I discovered all cross-Channel ferries had been cancelled thanks to Force Ten gales. For the previous two days, that is. Today it seemed luck was on my side. As I queued for a ticket, the Tannoy announced normal services were resuming. Thank fuck for that, I thought. The rational part of my brain was doing battle with the irrational – I knew my chances of being caught were small, but I couldn't help thinking I was going to get nicked any minute. Having to go home and sit it out till the storms had passed would have jangled my nerves no end.

I kept my head down at the station, adrenalin keeping me alert. In life, it's not very often you're conscious of existing moment to moment, and it's amazing how your senses prick up when you're on the lookout for danger. Everything's more intense. Sights and sounds are somehow magnified and you feel more alive than ever. Not that it's a particularly comfortable feeling, mind you, but it's an interesting experience.

Blending in with the crowd can be hard if you're feeling edgy – even the actor in me found it hard to discern whether my body language was giving the game away. One thing I did know was that talking to people is always an excellent way to avoid looking conspicuous – it seemed to work in countless espionage movies I'd seen, anyway. So I thought I'd give that a try. Taking my seat on the Dover train, I smiled at the couple sitting across from me and soon enough we got chatting.

They were a lovely young couple from Mexico City, on their way to Paris, capital of romance, to begin their gap year in Europe. Their English wasn't great, but we managed to hold a decent enough conversation. I spun a yarn about my reasons for visiting Paris, and we stuck together boarding the ferry at Dover. I admit I was using them as cover, and it worked. Nobody had looked at me twice when I passed through Customs.

I hadn't eaten all day, and they were hungry too, so we headed for the ferry's restaurant. The three of us soon steamed into the only food on offer: bacon and eggs. I fancied a drink to calm my nerves, and the Mexicans were game too because, well, they were young and in love. The trouble was the only tipple on offer was rosé wine. What the hell, we thought, and ordered a bottle.

Our meal went down well enough, but we realised we'd made a big mistake as soon as the ferry cleared the harbour and hit open sea. The gales had moved on, but the weather was still stormy enough to toss the ferry around like a kid's boat in a bathtub. And it wasn't long before my breakfast made its way back whence it came. I was so sick, and I wasn't alone. I don't think one person on that ferry came off lightly. The poor Mexicans were in bits. It was the worst ferry crossing ever. I was ready to kiss the ground when we got to the other side, and to this day I've never again touched a drop of rosé.

After recovering on the Calais to Paris train, I bid goodbye to the Mexicans and made my way across Gay Paree to Charles de Gaulle Airport. I needed a flight to Madrid and tried every airline besides British Airways (who always made a record of any British travellers), all to no avail. I couldn't believe my bad luck. There were tons of flights to Madrid, but not one fucking seat. I was 22, it was the first time I'd been abroad alone *and* I was on the lam, so understandably there were a few moments when I felt a twinge of rising panic. I'd been given a plan and told not to veer from it, but what was I to do now? Sticking to what I'd been told could mean waiting around a couple of days, perhaps more, and that was the last thing I wanted. Still, it seemed I had no other option.

I tried yet another airline desk, only to face another steward telling me there were *definitely* no seats to Madrid. Then I felt a hand on my shoulder. I froze.

'Excuse me, sir,' came an English a voice. Oh, God, I thought, I've drawn attention to myself. I've been spotted. Expecting the worst, I turned around.

'There's a train, you know,' said a friendly-looking man.

'A what?' I said, gathering my composure, reeling with relief. This bloke was no copper – it seemed he was just trying to help.

'A train from here to Madrid. Perhaps you could try that.'

It sounded good to me. I'd already had enough of the airport – I was edgy and desperate to keep moving. I thanked the bloke, got the hell out of Charles de Gaulle and hailed a cab to the Gare d'Austerlitz.

Train ticket in hand, I passed nervously through a

security checkpoint with only a cursory glance at my passport and headed for the platform. Thankfully, there were plenty of seats on the train, and as I sat down I breathed a tiny sigh of relief. What a beautiful train it was. I'd never seen anything like it. Everything was new and streamlined and the seats were big and comfortable. Pure class – a far cry from British Rail. Nervous as I'd been, the luxury and romance of my surroundings did wonders for my state of mind. In a matter of hours I'd gone from grotty old Victoria to this. I was back on track – literally.

So far, so good. By now part of me was enjoying playing the part of a Frenchman at leisure – or a British agent on a mission. I know it may sound silly, but thinking like that really helped me. It kept me sharp.

I began to relax a little when the train glided into motion and slowly pulled out of the station. Looking out of the window, I said goodbye to the Paris I'd had no time to take in. An overwhelming feeling hit me as the train snaked further through the suburbs. Hunger. I hadn't eaten since that bacon and eggs on the boat, and that lot hadn't stayed down long. Cigarettes and nerves had kept me going, and only now did I realise I was running on empty. It was time to refuel.

Entering the dining carriage was like stepping on to a film set – it was a beautiful little car filled with people puffing plumes of blue Gauloise smoke, drinking red wine and coffee, animatedly talking and eating what the French do best – *Steak Frites*. All the cuts were laid out for customers to pick from, and I didn't waste any time in choosing a perfect-looking steak and handing it to a chef.

I took a seat, sipped my glass of red and gazed out of the window. The lush French countryside opened up all around as the train rattled along. Every second I was further away from home, yet closer to where I wanted to be. I'm doing all right, I thought. I'd refined the plan a little, sure. But I'd got this far. All in all I felt the situation couldn't get much better. I soon discovered I was wrong when I laid eyes on a lovely-looking French girl and realised she had her eyes flirtatiously locked on me. A beautiful girl to pass the time with – fantastic. It *doesn't* get better than that.

She was a petite brunette with a lovely round mouth and big, doll-like eyes. We made eyes at each other and exchanged a few words of broken French and English. A very pleasant distraction, our flirtation kept me busy all the way to the French–Spanish border, high in the Pyrenees. But arriving at a place where my plan might be thwarted brought me right back down to earth.

It was the middle of the night. The train hissed, whirred, then fell silent. I disembarked into the freezing mountain air and huddled along the platform. Only the sound of shuffling feet broke the silence as I stood in line for French passport control. I clutched my passport and prayed. There was no reason why I should be stopped, but once again my irrational fears kicked in. The Foremans hadn't been too lucky with Customs of late. '*What if...?*' said that demon in my head.

As it turned out, the Customs men were only on the lookout for migrant workers trying to sneak into France illegally. Presumably I didn't fit the migrant bill looks-wise, for as I passed through the officers waved me on with a mere glance at my passport. It was the same story on the Spanish side. A nice stroke of luck. I'd moved from France to Spain without my name being noted on any document, and it felt good. Looking back, getting the train was probably an even smarter move than taking a plane – you didn't need your name on the ticket for rail travel. To all intents and purposes, I'd disappeared off the radar.

I'd come from a British winter, but even I wasn't prepared for the frigid cold of the Spanish mountains at night. Stomping my feet and hugging myself for warmth, I waited on another platform for my next train. The French girl was standing nearby and I kept my eye on her as I lit another cigarette. Noticing me puffing away, an American student approached and asked if I had a spare cigarette. I gave him a whole packet out of a carton I'd bought, and we got talking. Nodding towards a group of kids further down the platform, he told me they were all heading to the south of Spain for the winter. 'What you up to, man?' he enquired casually.

'Oh, just bumming around for a bit,' I said. It was

obvious these friendly young kids weren't in cahoots with MI5, but I had to stay on my guard.

'Well, why don't you come and spend Christmas with us? We've got a beautiful house on the beach just outside Malaga.'

I looked over to the group of students. Among them were a couple of very tasty-looking girls who weren't shy about throwing me some gorgeous smiles – it wasn't hard to picture myself enjoying Christmas on the beach with that lot. I thanked the bloke for his offer, saying I might well join them. I scribbled down the address, knowing I would never use it. Then I looked over at the girls again. If only, I thought. If only.

The train that pulled into the station was worlds apart from the sleek TGV number I'd sped through France on. A rickety little thing made mostly of wood, it looked like something from the Wild West. Everyone was freezing, and couldn't wait to board the train. The doors opened and within seconds the previously sedate crowd became a bunch of desperadoes. It was bedlam with all the pushing and shoving. I was aghast to see people actually fighting to get on a train.

I spotted the little French girl struggling in the middle of it all. She was being jostled out of the way by grown men. Well, I wasn't having any of that. I barged my way over to her, wrapped her in my arms and hurled her up on to the train. I threw my case up to her and jumped on. We were safe.

So much for escaping the cold – the seating compartments were like ice. It turned out the heating system was knackered, and much to everyone's irritation the guards soon came round and slung us all off the train. After all that effort, we were back where we started. The crazy thing was the same train pulled up at the platform half an hour later. Another scrum ensued, but this time I minded the girl from the off. Once seated back in the same compartment, we realised the heating hadn't been fixed at all. You've got to love the Spanish. It's funny now, but we weren't laughing then.

Still, the lack of heat wasn't all bad – before I knew it the girl had snuggled up and put her head on my shoulder. I covered us with my jacket and gave her a protective cuddle as the train heaved out of the station. We had a bit of a kiss when the lights were eventually turned out for the night, and at one point we slipped off for a bit more *privacy*. It came as a very welcome interlude after all the stress I'd been through. *Merci, Mam'selle.* Being on the run, having a brief encounter with a gorgeous French girl and falling into a deep sleep on a train plunging ever deeper into the heart of Spain – it was like I was living in a novel. Pure romance and adventure.

There's nothing like sleeping through the night and waking to find you're somewhere else, still on the move. As I came to, the first thing I noticed was the heat. It was baking. A wonderful contrast to the biting cold of the mountain air. Looking out of the window, my eyes met with the barren dryness of Spain's northern plains. A far cry from the Pyrenees, the flat landscape spread out as far as the eye could see. I threw off my jacket and opened the window. I was in the middle of nowhere. I'll never forget the feeling of that hot, dry air on my face and the sense that with every moment I was drawing nearer to safety.

Gently, I shook my little French friend awake and gave her a soft kiss on the cheek. She rubbed her sleepy eyes and we smiled at each other. It was time for breakfast. The buffet car was a true antiquity. Wood-panelled walls and banquettes. I almost expected to come under attack from redskins riding alongside the train shooting arrows at us. I let mademoiselle take the reins when it came to ordering and soon we were tucking into bread, jam, croissants and black coffee – a truly continental way to begin the day. I watched as she dipped a croissant into her coffee. I'd never seen that before, but gave it a go. Delicious. I still do that to this day.

All good things come to an end – or at least they had to in my circumstances. When the train pulled into Madrid, I knew it was time for goodbyes. Funnily enough, I discovered the girl was on her way to meet her boyfriend – those French girls, eh! – but we exchanged addresses anyway and parted company. It had been short but sweet. As I lugged my suitcase off to the taxi rank, I knew our paths would never cross again.

When I ran into trouble in Paris, I managed to find an alternative to flying. Now, in Madrid, I was too far from the coast to find another mode of transport to Tenerife. This time it was a flight or nothing. It was the festive season, and my heart sank when I realised the place was rammed with Spaniards jetting off for Christmas. Weaving my way through the midday deluge, I prayed I'd be able to get on a plane and complete the final leg of my journey.

No such luck. All flights were fully booked. Fuck. All I could do was put my name (false, of course) down for a standby seat, sit down and wait. Four flights departed for Tenerife without me, the last one taking off early evening. I wasn't happy, to put it mildly. There was nothing for it, I'd have to stay the night and try again in the morning. Double fuck.

It turned out I was in for a long night. I was anxious enough, but might have got a few hours' sleep in my chair were it not for a gang of dodgy-looking *gitanos* – gypsies – lurking around the airport. I'd clocked them early on and it was obvious they were eyeing up all the suitcases in the hope of an easy touch. Watching them prowl around, I was convinced I'd wake up without my luggage if I dozed off, so I didn't sleep a wink. Those *gitanos* gave me the evil eye all night. Finally, I'd had enough. Risking bringing attention to myself, I caught the leader's eye and made it perfectly clear that if they fancied their chances they should come and have a try.

They must have appreciated my *cojones*, for the leader nodded and smiled. From then on they left me alone. Still, I remained awake. By daybreak I was deranged with tiredness and so irritable I was ready to explode.

The first flight was 8am, and in my mind I was getting on that plane no matter what. When the desk opened I was right at the front, ready to tell the booking steward what was what. 'I've been waiting here since yesterday lunchtime,' I shouted, 'and it's my turn to leave.' Having been passed over in favour of some Spaniards earlier, I'd had enough. Finally, I got a seat. I boarded the plane and as soon as I sat down I fell asleep, exhausted.

An hour later I emerged into the sweltering heat of San Antonio Airport. I'd made it. A flight from London would have got me there in a couple of hours, while my adventure had taken just over two days. I pulled out the hidden piece of paper the chaps had given me, dialled the number and was told to head to a certain bar in Los Cristianos. I hailed a cab. As we bounced along the road, it struck me that there were only a couple of people in the world who knew my whereabouts. I'd disappeared. Mission accomplished.

What a magnificent and slightly surreal moment it was when I walked into the bar, looked around and spotted my mum, sister and Dad. As always, there was the beaming smile, the arms spread wide. Same old Fred, taking his surroundings in his stride. 'We've been so worried about you. What took you so long?' I couldn't begin to tell them. I was just so relieved to have made it. I'd recount my story later. What I needed right then was a very large drink.

We had a *good* drink. Suddenly, it was as if the past few days hadn't happened. I sat back and basked in the wonderful moment – my family back together. I passed Dad some money he was owed, along with some messages from the chaps, and eventually asked him what had been happening.

The flat answer was 'not much'. Back in the seventies Los Cristianos was only a tiny resort – more of a glorified fishing village really – and there wasn't much to do there. You didn't see many English people. Most of the tourists were Germans and Swedes, and that's precisely why Dad chose it as a place to lay low. The Brits tended to congregate a few miles away at Playa de Las Americas, and that suited us fine.

Dad had rented a lovely apartment overlooking the beach. It was a good spot, but not quite big enough – I had to sleep on the sofa most of the time, which became irritating. Still, it was nicely out of the way and we were under no obligation to do anything. Life resembled being on holiday, but we all had to keep a bit of an alert on the whole time. I arrived just before Christmas, and it was bizarre and lovely having our Christmas lunch on a terrace in the blazing heat.

Being at leisure abroad for an extended period may sound quite exciting, but having to keep a low profile in a foreign country is one of the most boring things in the world. Trust me. Granted, lounging about on a beach is a good deal better than getting nicked and being banged up, but psychologically you're still somewhere you don't want to be. Knowing you *have* to be there turns it into a strange sort of prison sentence.

Being away put pressure on us as a family, Dad in particular. Once again he was very conscious of living on limited money now he'd cut loose from business in London – though we regularly received Dad's share of the pool-table money thanks to Teddy Dennis. We all had our moments of frustration, so now and again a row would flare up, but we never lost sight of how lucky we were to be together as a family. It could have been a hundred times worse if the chaps hadn't acted fast and whisked Dad away, and we'll be forever grateful to those wonderful, canny individuals. True friends.

There wasn't much to occupy us, and nothing I could do to change that. I missed acting hugely and remember feeling totally starved creatively. Unable to pursue my first passion, I did the next best thing: I read. I sat on the beach and devoured any book I could get my hands on. I can hardly remember all the books I read, but I remember ploughing through all of Stephen King's novels. *The Shining* completely blew me away. I remember visualising Jack Nicholson as the protagonist, so it was no surprise when he was cast in Kubrick's amazing film version. I also discovered the joy of John le

Carré's work. It was in Tenerife that I really fell in love with his wonderfully vivid prose, the depth of his characters and the amazing structure of his novels. To this day he's my favourite author. Some of his early work may have suffered from being over-described, but since *Tinker, Tailor* his writing just glides. In my humble opinion he's only got better over the years. He's also matured well – the sign of a true artist. I like to think I've done the same with my acting. My favourite novel is *A Perfect Spy*, probably because of the parallels with my own childhood (a father in prison, a child at boarding school). Not that I would ever commit treason – that would be as bad as grassing.

It was rare to hear an English voice in Los Cristianos, and we all got by in the pidgin Spanish we'd acquired, mostly from the television. Our favourite programme was *Los Angeles de Charlie* – I'll leave you to work that one out. Dad was constantly in touch with the chaps back home, but the word was always the same: 'wait'. We were better off where we were. The weeks seemed interminable and passed mostly without incident. That changed suddenly one day when we all headed down to the beach as usual.

'Freddie!' came a voice. A very loud, London voice.

We all stopped dead in our tracks, and I'll never forget the way Dad's eyes widened as he turned with a nervous grimace. Was this it? Was the game up? We'd all been so careful for months, surely the cops weren't on us now.

My heart raced as we turned, but I let out a sigh of relief when I saw who'd called out. It was good old Billy Backhouse, husband to Kathy, Ronnie Oliffe's sister. In the past I had been out drinking with their two sons, Danny and Tony. 'Billy!' Dad shouted back, but not quite so loudly. 'Good to see you.' And it was. They were on holiday with their friends Bernie and Rose, and to us they were from decent stock, as good as family. It wasn't ideal we'd been spotted, but what better people to have seen us.

After four months with no one but each other to really talk to, it was a novel event to be talking to people we shared a background with. I'm sure Dad would have preferred it if nobody ever saw us, but even he was happy once he realised our chance encounter was with such staunch friends. It was a proper break from the norm, as if a pressure valve had just been opened.

Billy Backhouse had a reputation for being a bit of a prankster, and that day he didn't waste any time living up to it. Back home he was a docker but he also did a lot of work for charity and loved dressing up to raise money. Billy also enjoyed putting on a costume just for laughs, and he and his wife Kathy had a hilarious little routine they did on the beach. Kathy went into the sea for a swim, while Billy nipped off to get changed. Minutes later you saw him marching down the beach, braying and growling in a Frankenstein costume and making all the kids scream with delight. Then he'd wade into the sea and haul Kathy out while the whole beach looked on. Nobody knew it was his wife, and she'd scream for help in his arms before cracking a big smile and giving Frankenstein a hug.

We all fell about laughing as Billy stomped back up to our spot in the sand. Bernie had a music box, and switched it on loud before Frankenstein and his maiden began to dance. It was a class act, and people loved the performance. The only trouble was tons of holidaymakers got their cameras out and began snapping away. Ever since arriving, Dad had told us to make sure we had our faces covered or heads turned whenever pictures were being taken, and we'd got pretty sharp at keeping away from other people's lenses. You never knew who was going to see those photos – believe it or not, I know people who've been on the run and got nicked as a result of a copper looking at a pal's holiday snaps. It wasn't hard to look the other way in bars and restaurants, but being on a beach surrounded by people was a different story. We had no choice but to duck our heads towards the sand and wait until it was all over. We used to laugh at the thought of people looking at their photos and always seeing this family with their backs turned.

We couldn't have bumped into better people to cheer us up. Billy and Kathy stayed for two weeks and, knowing they'd never say a word about it back home, we had lunch with them every day. During those times I really felt like we were on holiday and almost managed to forget why we were holed up in Tenerife. It was heaven to have other people to talk to, and that fortnight broke up the monotony of everything. I know that it was a real tonic for my mum to have Kathy and Rose to talk to. Women do need other women to share their thoughts and frustrations with. I couldn't have been happier seeing her deep in conversation with the girls, laughing and unloading the stress she was undoubtedly under.

A very strange thing happened during our stay. One night Danielle woke up in the middle of the night and went to the bathroom. For some reason she felt compelled to pull the shower curtain open, and what she saw next was truly astonishing. An apparition of a man was standing in the bathtub. It was Dukey. The shock of it made Danielle jump, but a strange calm soon descended on her. Suddenly she wasn't scared, and knew she wasn't in danger: Dukey had a big smile on his face that reassured her all was well. She stared, stunned and mesmerised, hardly able to believe her eyes. But there was more. Moments later Dukey began to speak.

'Tell your Mum and Dad I'm happy,' he said. 'Tell them everything's all right. I'm very happy and that I'm sorry for the problems I caused you. I never wanted that. Tell everyone I love them...'

And then he was gone.

Danielle rushed to wake us all. Hearing her story, we were gobsmacked. We believed everything she told us.

Mum in particular believed in such phenomena, and my dad's experiences with the old ghost down the Marshalsea Road premises had made him a convert. Although I had never experienced the supernatural, I hadn't ruled out the possibility of its existence. Danielle's experience had a profound effect on all of us. Knowing that Duke was all right made us feel good, and it was very reassuring to think that he was watching over us. A very emotional moment, it got me reflecting on the magnitude of the events that had led to our current situation.

Being reminded of Dukey's tragic fate made me realise how very lucky we were to be together – it didn't matter how frustrating being away had sometimes been. God rest Dukey's soul, I thought. Little did I know it wasn't the last time a strange reminder of Pasha would enter my life.

Our escape to Tenerife was only ever a temporary measure. Back home, the chaps had been working to arrange a longer-term solution for us. We'd been away six months when Dad got word it was time to move on again – the chaps had heard a whisper that the police believed they knew our location. We weren't told where we would move to – not yet – but it was made clear that Dad needed to return to England briefly before slipping away again. We would follow. This was music to my ears after all those tedious months in Tenerife.

Dad travelled back on his fake passport, while the rest

of us returned through a package deal, pretending we were tourists. The cops still wanted me, I was told, but after six months the situation wasn't as hot. I didn't need to retrace my steps through Spain and France. The authorities knew I'd disappeared and we reasoned they wouldn't be expecting me to turn up. The package deal made us look like a family on holiday, and back then all the electronic systems Customs have nowadays didn't exist – by the time any paper records of my arrival got to anyone who'd be interested, I would have already disappeared again.

Within a couple of days of Dad going, we bid goodbye to the island and said hello to home sweet home. We got back to drizzly autumnal Britain, all of us tanned up to the eyeballs after months of baking heat. There was no way we could return to South London, so we were kindly accommodated by a relative in Gidea Park, Romford.

It was a huge relief to be back, even if it was only a flying visit. But it was frustrating being stuck out in Essex and knowing my beloved London was tantalisingly close. I spent a couple days feeling so near to the wonderful life I'd known, yet at the same time so far. Of course I couldn't bowl up and show my face all over town, but I wondered if I might get away with just one low-key visit. Out of everyone I'd missed, there was one friend I desperately wanted to say hello to.

Could I risk a couple of hours in town for a brief taste of the old days? I wondered. After a chat with Mum, we decided the risk was low enough. Dad had already slipped out of the country again and we didn't know where he'd gone. If the worst happened, and I got nicked, I'd be a useless sprat for catching that mackerel.

Pandy was the man I wanted to see. We are like brothers, and I'd never said goodbye before Tenerife. Back then we'd always gone to Pizza Express in Dean Street – the flagship restaurant that's still there today – for a catch-up and a meal whenever I was in town. If I was going to see him again, there was no better place for our brief reunion. I picked up the phone.

'Hello, mate,' I said brightly. 'Fancy a pizza?' It had always been my line with Pandy.

'Mate!' he exclaimed, knowing better than to use my name. 'Fucking hell. Of course!'

I didn't need to tell him where, just when – 1pm the next day. That call was a fantastic moment. For a second it was as if I'd never been away.

Travelling into London the next day, I felt the inevitable nerves and at odd moments wondered if re-entering the lion's den was a little audacious, a touch foolish. Perhaps I was dicing with my liberty, but looking back I think I needed to do it for my own sanity. I'd hardly been in the company of anyone outside of my own family for six months. I knew I'd be leaving the country again soon – God knows how long for this time – and it would have broken my heart not to have a glimpse of home before I moved on to unknown territory.

I got the train to Liverpool Street Station, then the tube to Soho. I stole through the side streets, being careful to avoid the main thoroughfares, but making sure I had a peek down the streets that held an infinity of fond memories. Shaftesbury Avenue, Charing Cross Road and Tin Pan Alley were all there, of course, and all the same. I didn't want to bump into anyone I knew, so kept my head down. How I would have loved to pop into the A & R for a drink, just like Dad and I used to.

Good old London had carried on unchanged. People rushed around lost in their own worlds, and I gazed on like an invisible man. I could look but I couldn't touch. All the memories were there, but I wasn't in a position to go out and make any more. I could allow myself one thing, though: a seat in the corner of my favourite pizza place. I shrugged off my ennui, made my way there and ordered a drink.

Seeing Pandy was magic. We beamed at each other as he walked over, and caught up on everything that had been going on. He wanted to know where I'd been, how I'd been and how come I looked so well with that golden suntan. I said as much as I could and told him all about Los Cristianos – I figured it didn't matter any more. I added that I'd soon be on my travels again, but that I didn't know where to.

Then it was my turn to ask the questions. How was everyone? How was Pandy's family? How was Nick? And what about John Bunce's sex life? Pandy filled me in on everything, and said that people had been asking after me. He had covered for me, though, simply telling people I was fine and working out of London. Good old Pandy. I felt like I'd been gone an age – when you're living a normal life, six months is nothing, but six months on the lam is a different matter – and a simple pizza and a few beers with a true friend was just the tonic for a man who'd been so lonely while away. My family were always wonderful, but your flesh and blood can't always be a substitute for your mates, and vice versa.

I knew I was going away again, but this time I got to tell my best mate and say goodbye. Pandy wouldn't be left wondering what had become of me, nor did I have to act as if nothing was amiss. That brief lunch meant the world, and I knew we'd meet again someday.

As I headed back to Romford I knew that, no matter what was in store for me, I was ready to stand tall for my family, face the music and dance.

12

ACROSS THE POND

I had no idea where Dad was. None of us did. It was a case of everybody staying true to the old 'need to know basis' philosophy. We knew he was a long way away, and safe, and that was all that mattered. His whereabouts would be disclosed at an appropriate time. For the time being all we could do was sit tight and wait for the chaps to give us our instructions.

Not that we didn't spend hours speculating about where we'd end up joining Dad. We didn't have much else to do while sitting about in Romford – no disrespect, but it's not the most exciting of places. Mum, Danielle and I would watch the holiday programmes and daydream about where we would end up. Australia,

Hawaii, Haiti, and the Bahamas were right up there on the list.

Don't ask me why, but we never considered the possibility that Dad wouldn't be somewhere sunny – I suppose we assumed the next stop would resemble our Tenerife experience in some way. We couldn't have been further from the truth. Forget the palm trees and cocktails on the beach. It turned out Dad was bedded down in a little place called Allentown, Pennsylvania, in the good old US of A. Allen*where*? I thought. I'd never heard of it, not even in the movies. It didn't matter. The main thing was the Foremans were off to America, land of the free.

I was as happy as can be. I *loved* America. But my affection was based purely on what I'd seen at the movies or read in books, as it was for so many Brits back then. I was an avid film-goer who'd been saturated by American culture for years, and the idea of finally seeing the greatness of the States set my soul on fire. I imagined it would be great, anyway. I couldn't wait. Even though I was going on the run, part of me even fantasised there might be an opportunity to get my acting career going there. My mind buzzed with all the possibilities. As it turned out, I'd have plenty of other things to think about during my time away. But a bit of dreaming never does anyone any harm, does it?

It was decided I'd go first. Getting me out of the way was the most important thing, and Mum and Danielle would move over once I'd helped Dad establish a good place for us to live in. Meanwhile, Mum had the awful task of settling our affairs. Not knowing how long we were going to be away, my poor mother was left the very unhappy job of putting our beautiful house and contents up for sale. Dulwich had been our sanctuary when we left the pub, and it broke Mum's heart having to sell off all the gorgeous antique furniture she had collected over the years. The funds from selling the house and contents would bankroll our new life in America. That must have been the hardest, most terrible thing for Mum.

I didn't need to worry about the journey – once again the chaps had my route planned out down to the very last detail. I expected another 'this is what you do' speech was on its way, and I wasn't disappointed.

'Now this is what you do,' began Hands, his eyes locked on mine. 'You get a flight to New York. From JFK you get a cab to the Port Authority.'

New York! I thought, I like the sound of that.

Learning lines is an acquired skill, and I have a natural flair for it, but I'd never been in a play where my fate and liberty rested on not getting a word wrong. I could always read a script more than once, but this was *real* life and I had to commit every word to memory on first time of hearing. I listened intently to the rest of the plan to get me to Allentown, and repeated it back perfectly.

'Well done,' said Hands flatly. 'And remember. Do not

use the phone; not to home, not to anyone. Once you get there, sit tight and you'll be picked up within a few days.'

'There' was the George Washington Motel in Allentown. My final destination. Hands gave me a plane ticket and $1,000 in cash and wished me luck.

Going on my toes to America was exciting, but saying goodbye to Mum and Danielle was a tearful moment. We'd been relatively safe in Romford, but moving around again meant showing my face at borders and Customs and having my name recorded on paper. We all knew anything might happen, and our farewells brought all that worry to the surface. Still, it did us good to let some emotion out – we'd all stayed so strong for so long in order to protect each other, but sometimes a tear or two can bring a family even closer. I gave my Danni a big hug and asked her to look after Mum.

'Look after yourself, my love,' said Mum. Like all good mothers, she always fretted over her son. I told her she didn't have to worry. I'd done it before and I'd do it again. That said, if there's one thing in life that doesn't get any easier with practice, it's travelling on your toes as a wanted man. No matter how tight your plan is, nor how many times you've succeeded in the past, your mind never rests until you've got where you need to be.

The old fears were back. Was I being followed? Would I get spotted? Might I get pulled aside by Customs at Heathrow? Would there be any awkward questions once

I landed in America? I didn't have the slightest clue. My deepest fear was that the authorities would be on to me but holding back until I led them to Dad, the man they really wanted. It didn't bear thinking about. The idea of exposing my father sent shivers down my spine and strengthened my resolve to be extra vigilant. All I could do was accept my worries would plague me till the two of us were together in a room, and behind a door that wasn't being broken down.

Everything went smoothly, to begin with at least. I had my story ready in case of any questions – I was a young actor heading for New York to look for a bit of work and meet some new people – but nobody batted an eyelid as I strolled through Customs at Heathrow. I was courteous as ever at passport control, where the bloke at the desk let me through with a smile. Perfect. Roll on, the Big Apple.

I had no trouble at JFK either, and within an hour of landing I was cruising along in my first-ever yellow cab, driven by an eccentric, chatty Polack who must have been one of the biggest blokes I'd ever encountered. How I wished I really was on a trip to act and meet people. I would have done anything to spend some time taking in the city that had always captured my imagination. But, alas, it was not to be. Another time, I thought, my eyes darting everywhere to glimpse the sights I'd seen a thousand times on the big screen. I recalled the way my hero Sinatra sung 'New York, New

York', and, boy, did I want to be a part of it. And for a brief time, as the cab headed downtown and through Manhattan, I suppose I was. At the same time 'Living for the City' by Stevie Wonder came to mind. Stevie sings about a poor sap who arrives in the city that never sleeps and winds up getting nicked and sent to jail. That won't be me, I thought.

The cabbie pulled up and turned his huge frame towards me. 'I'm guessing you haven't been to the Port Authority before,' he said in a broad Bronx accent. He was right, of course.

I shook my head.

'Take it from me,' he growled. 'It's not a nice place in there. You don't talk to anyone unless they are in a uniform, and you don't let go of your case once. Hold on to it, and keep your head down, got it?'

I got it all right – a few minutes ago I'd been caught up in the romance of everything, and now I had the fear of God instilled in me. Still, I was grateful to the Polack for his no-bullshit advice. I soon realised he hadn't exaggerated.

'Not a nice place,' he'd said. What an understatement. The bus terminal was a proper hell-hole. Filled with layabouts, junkies and hustlers, it reminded me of King's Cross Station back home. From the moment I walked in I was fending off one chancer after another. Even though I'd always been able to handle myself, it was still very intimidating. At least I could tell I wasn't being followed – an undercover cop would have stood out a mile in this crowd. I certainly did – I must have been the only white bloke in there. All eyes were on me as I jostled through the throng towards the ticket desk.

An Allentown bus was leaving in half an hour. Thank fuck for that, I thought. I didn't want to spend a minute more than I had to in this piss-hole. I felt like a settler being surrounded by hostile Indians. To one side was a café area. Head for the pass, I thought. I found a pitch at the end of the counter and put my case behind me against the wall as if to say, 'You want it, come and get it.' Fending off the vultures, I felt like I was back in Madrid Airport again. Show no fear, I told myself.

I ordered a hot dog – my first taste of Americana. I've never ever eaten a meal with so many people glaring at me. One after another, the dodgiest-looking hustlers on the planet asked me if I needed any help. Help with what? Being robbed blind? My answers were short and sharp. There was no way I was taking any shit from these lowlifes. Naturally, the announcement of my bus came as a very welcome relief.

As I boarded the Greyhound for Allentown, I began to relax a little. I'd made it this far, and now I was on the last leg of my journey. It was the middle of the night so the bus wasn't even half full. The engine started, the bus pulled away and the bright lights of New York City were soon behind us. I gazed out of the window at the flat, snow-covered landscapes of New Jersey and north-east Pennsylvania and marvelled at the infinity of bright stars hanging in the black sky. Eventually, we passed through our first small town, and every town after that felt like a déjà vu. They all looked identical: Same gas station. Same diner. Same shops. Same pizza parlour. Same fucking everything. Absolutely no individuality.

I was filled with nervous excitement as I headed further into the unknown. So far the chaps' plan had gone like clockwork. After a couple of days in Allentown, I'd be picked up and taken to my father. I couldn't wait to get there. The bus only stopped a few times. As it stole onwards in the darkness, a song kept playing over and over in my head: Paul Simon's 'Homeward Bound'. I think it was the line about standing at a railroad station with a ticket for a destination that got me humming it, and the tune stayed with me for the whole journey. Thinking about it, although I'd left Mum and Danielle back in England, I was nonetheless bound for the place that would become my new home, so a song about longing for home was pretty apt, whichever way you look at it. These days hearing the track always evokes such vivid memories of that journey.

It was around midnight when another town loomed out of the blackness. Again it looked no different from all the others. The only difference was this place had a motel on the outskirts called the George Washington – I saw it out of the corner of my eye as the bus headed downtown. Blimey, I thought, *this* is Allentown. Finally I'd arrived.

'That's it, folks,' said the bus driver, switching off the engine. 'Final stop.'

The few remaining passengers shuffled off the bus and disappeared into the night. I was the last to descend on to the deserted street. The first thing to hit me was the cold. It was well below freezing and all I had on was a thin shirt, chinos, loafers and a little suede jacket. I began to shiver instantly. Plumes of condensation enveloped me as I exhaled. Looking around, I noticed the snow piled up, shoulder high, at the edge of the pavement. The town was dead. Neon lights reflected on the wet streets, and it looked like an empty film set. Fucking hell, I thought. What the hell am I doing here? And, if this is where he is, what about Dad?

My motel was quite a way back, and there was no way I could have walked there. I would have frozen. I asked the bus driver where I could get a cab.

'You'll have to drop a dime and call one,' he said, nodding towards a phone booth. 'There should be a sign with a number in there.'

It was my first time in an American phone booth. Feeling like an actor in my very own road movie, I fumbled for the ten cents and punched in the number. The wind picked up and whipped a flurry of snow around the booth, and someone answered. Through chattering teeth I asked how long the wait for a cab would be. The answer came right away: two hours.

Bollocks. This was certainly no swinging metropolis – more like a one-horse town.

I hurried back to the bus stop and asked the driver if there were any buses.

'Where are you going?' he asked casually.

I hesitated. Throughout my journey I hadn't told a soul where I was heading. 'Trust no one' was my motto. But what was I to do now? Reality was biting along with the cold, and if I wanted to avoid frostbite I'd have to take a chance. Besides, I thought, what did a bus driver care who I was?

As I suspected he might, the driver said there were no buses running this late. Then, just when I was about to tear my hair out, I was served a slice of American goodwill. 'I'll tell you what,' he said, 'I'm heading back to the depot to pick my car up, but I'll drop you off after. Jump back on.'

Hailing from London, it came as a real shock that a bus driver would bother helping me out. But sometimes the kindness of strangers can really take you by surprise. That night, out of the goodness of his heart, a man saved my bacon. It was a lovely thing to do and I'll never forget that touching moment. It was quite a drive to the depot and we had a good chat. I bluffed my way out of the inevitable 'so what brings you here?' and, by the time we bid each other farewell outside the motel, I realised there was no way I could have made it there under my own steam.

I was at the end of the road. Thousands of miles were behind me and I was exhausted. I checked in. Hats off to the chaps – they'd found me a corker of a motel. It was a beautiful, lodge-style building, with a huge, welcoming fireplace and a dark-wood lounge. There was a bar and a restaurant and even a heated indoor swimming pool. I'll be using that in the morning, I thought. But right then all I wanted was rest. I ordered a couple of sodas, took them to my room, flopped on to the bed and switched on the telly. The first programme that came on was *Soap*, an American sitcom I'd been watching in the UK – a strange reminder of home. I flipped channels. There was a Sinatra film playing. How many times had I watched my hero Frank on TV back home? I reckoned it was a good omen. I smiled to myself. Welcome to America, Jamie, I thought, and drifted off.

It is really draining when you have been living on your nerves. After a much-needed sleep, I awoke the next morning and headed to the dining room for my first American breakfast. I'd not eaten since that hot dog, and I was ravenous.

I ordered eggs, bacon and some lovely-looking potato hash. The waitress called it 'scrapple'.

'How do you want your eggs?' she asked.

'Over easy,' I said, just like in the films. I didn't have a clue what it meant, but had always loved the phrase. It turned out I loved the eggs when they came – 'over easy' meant cooked on both sides and nice and runny. Perfect.

This is the life, I thought, and dipped my toast in the yolk. I smiled at the waitress as she topped up my coffee. Ensconced in a motel in the middle of nowhere, I felt safe for the first time in days. All I had to do now was wait a day or two to be collected. I had plenty of dollars left, so there was nothing to worry about on that front. The only drawback was I couldn't leave the motel in case I was contacted, but at least it was a comfortable place to sit tight.

I didn't want to talk to many people, but there was a pretty girl on reception and I couldn't resist having a little flirt with her. She was full of that apple-pie friendliness and told me all about my new surroundings. Turned out Allentown wasn't such a small place after all, but more of a small city of a couple of hundred thousand. The motel was on the edge of town, and the nearest big cities were New York to the north, Philadelphia to the south and Atlantic City to the east.

Known as 'The Little Apple', Allentown had everything you'd expect from a small city, and Billy Joel had even written a song about it. Unfortunately, I'd have to wait before I ventured into it. Still, I told the receptionist – sadly I can't remember her name – I would love her to show me around. She didn't say no. Interesting, I thought.

Nothing much happened on the first day. I took a swim, sat around and had myself a good lunch. In the afternoon I had a couple of drinks in the piano bar while listening to a half-decent jazz singer. It was good to be relaxing a bit, and since I had the cash I didn't feel bad when I treated myself to a good dinner later that evening. After another little flirtation with the lovely receptionist, it was TV and bed.

The next day was basically a repeat performance. But there is only so much sitting around on his own a man can do. By the afternoon I was starting to hope they'd pick me up sooner rather than later. Wherever he might be, I wanted to be with Dad and know all was well.

Day three. Still I didn't hear anything. I was bored as hell by now and starting to go a little stir crazy in the motel. I felt a little hint of anxiety start to creep in, but boredom can do that to you. I kept reminding myself that the chaps had said it might be up to four days. By mid-afternoon I was convinced nobody would be along that day and thought I might as well take a trip into town in the evening. Then I thought about the receptionist I'd been getting on so well with. She was heading off to see her folks the next day she told me, so it was now or never.

'What time do you finish your shift?' I asked her. Early enough, it turned out. She seemed as keen as me and readily agreed to let me take her out for dinner. It was a date. 'Fantastic,' I said. 'I would be broken-hearted if I didn't get a chance to buy you dinner. Let's go to your favourite restaurant,' I said. And that's what we did.

Allentown looked lovely that night. She told me the

Dutch had settled there a couple of hundred years back and I noticed some of the houses and buildings reflected that European look. It was heaven to get away from the motel and be distracted by a beautiful American girl. It turned out she was an aspiring artist. The job at the motel was only a means for her to indulge her passion for painting. We had a gorgeous meal – clams, broiled lobster tails and a not bad American Chardonnay – before ending the night at the motel. A very welcome little fling that ended the next day when she headed out of town.

Day four passed. Nothing. Same story on day five. By the time I put my head down that night, the anxiety was really starting to kick in. They know I'm here, I thought, so why leave me so long? Is something wrong? More frightening still, is it on me? Do the police know where I am? I consoled myself with the knowledge that the chaps always have their reasons. There was no way I would ever be abandoned. Never.

The next morning I had a roll-call on my finances and realised I was beginning to run out of money. Because I hadn't thought I'd be waiting around so long, I'd treated myself to a good few expensive meals. That would have to stop. No more lobster and steaks. From now on it would have to be pizza or KFC. But food was the least of my worries. It had been nearly a week now and I was starting to wonder what the fuck was happening.

I didn't have a clue where Dad was holed up and no

number to call him on. As darkness descended that night I felt very isolated, and not a little scared. After so many days alone my mind started to play tricks and paranoia crept in. It's definitely on me, I thought. The authorities know I'm here, and the chaps know the authorities know, so they're not coming near me. I've been followed and I'm done for. Please God, keep Dad away from me...

I mulled over the events of the past few days. Had I missed something, or someone? Had I let my guard down and failed to spot that I was under observation? Did I fuck up by letting that bus driver know where I was? Had I walked into a trap? I didn't have a clue, but I couldn't stop my mind buzzing with worry. Whatever the truth was, something was very wrong.

By day nine I had some serious decisions to make. I had sat it out patiently for nine days and now I had just a few dollars left in my pocket. The situation was getting desperate. I had only enough to stay in the motel another two nights, but I did have a return ticket to London. I began to wonder if flying home was the answer. If I stayed only one more night I would be left with just enough cash to get back to New York. It was one option, but having come this far I didn't want to turn back.

There was another option, though I didn't know how dangerous it was. I'd been warned not to make any phone calls. That would have been fine if the plan had worked, but what about now? Something had obviously fucked up, and unless I decided to abandon ship I had no choice but to put in a call to someone. I weighed up my choices, and decided to risk it. I thought carefully about who to call, eventually deciding on Uncle Fred. Fred was my mum's brother – a straight goer and good as gold. Surely there was no way the police would have tapped his phone.

He answered the phone almost immediately.

'Hello, Fred, it's me,' I said.

'Hello, mate,' he answered cheerily. Fred knew I was on the lam, but had no idea where I was. 'You all right?'

'No, I fucking ain't.' I was truly fed up. 'I need a favour. Can you go and see Hands and tell him I'm still here? Tell him I've run out of money and I don't know what to do next.'

Fred wasted no time, bless him. He got straight in his car and drove over to see Hands. Meanwhile, I paced around the room that had become my prison. The minutes ticked by and I wondered if I'd done the right thing. An hour later, I jumped at the noise when the bedside phone screamed – it was the first time I'd taken a call since checking in. I stared at it a second, then picked up.

'Jamie?' said a voice I didn't recognise in a heavy Glaswegian accent.

'Who's that?' I asked suspiciously.

Whoever it was started laughing raucously. I didn't feel like joining in.

'You poor fucker,' he said between guffaws. 'How long have you been here?'

'Nine fucking days.'

'Jesus! Pack your bag. I'll be round right away. Meet you in reception.'

Relief washed over me. I looked at the ceiling and let out a long breath. Thank you, God! I was safe and I was leaving. Minutes later, a beautiful Cadillac glided up and parked outside the motel. A ruggedly handsome, well-dressed Scotsman jumped out. His stocky frame rattled with laughter as he shook my hand and introduced himself. It was Joe MacLean. After everything I'd been through, I wasn't laughing. I actually felt like crying. It was such a huge relief to know the nightmare was finally over.

Joe squared up my bill and we drove off. I didn't waste any time in asking him what the hell had gone wrong. It turned out there'd been a breakdown in communication. My extended, anxiety-ridden stay at the motel was down to a man at the London end. Hands had told him to put a call in and say I was on my way, but the dozy bastard had somehow failed to pass the message on. As a result, Dad had spent the past few days as worried as me. God knows what would have happened if I hadn't phoned Uncle Fred.

Talking to Joe, I was astonished to discover how close we'd come to bumping into each other over the last few days. Dad and Joe had been moving around town and it turned out that a couple of days earlier they'd eaten at the same place as I had within minutes of my leaving. They'd even had breakfast at my motel. Each time we had missed each other by a whisker, which only made the situation seem so ludicrous.

More ludicrous still, Dad's apartment was only a couple of minutes' drive away. The Grecian Apollo condominium block was on a hill behind the George Washington Motel. All that time Dad had been just a hop, skip and a jump away. It made me angry to think the whole plan had nearly been thwarted by one dopey fool. This was serious business. People's liberty was at stake. I knew the bloke who'd fucked up would get a right bollocking for his sloppiness – that's the way it goes in Dad's world. There's no room for mistakes.

Joe pulled up outside the condo, and there stood Dad. Being in hiding is nerve-racking enough, but it really takes it out of you when a whole heap of unnecessary shit gets thrown into the mix. After the strain of the past few days, I can't describe how grateful I was to see my father's smiling face. I leaped out of the car and ran over to him. Relief overwhelmed us both as we hugged and kissed, a little watery-eyed with sheer emotion. Father and son were together again.

I'd made it across the Atlantic to my new home. My ordeal was finally over.

13

STARTING OVER

We needed to start over, as they say in America, but I wondered what on earth had brought Dad to Allentown. Tenerife had been a stopgap, but this time it was different. Dad needed to be away for a good while and put down some roots, and Allentown was the place we would remain for the foreseeable future. You couldn't have picked a place more different from London if you'd tried.

Talking to Dad, I discovered there was only one reason we'd ended up here: Joe MacLean. The laughing Glaswegian. Joe was an old mate of Dad's, one of the chaps, who'd moved to Allentown 14 years previously. He had been a big face on the Glasgow scene, but a gang war in the late sixties made his situation a little too hot to handle. Joe got out while the going was still good, moved to the US and rebuilt his life. He'd made a very good job of it too, establishing strong contacts with important local families, and going into business with Dave Rosen, a fantastic old man linked to some powerful New York crews. Known as Mr Philadelphia, Dave employed Joe to oversee his slot and games machine business, and Joe was bringing in some significant funds. He had even married a wonderful American girl, Joanne. She was a smart cookie and worked for a major company as the top exec's personal secretary. Joe and Dad had never lost touch, and Joe was only too happy to help when he discovered Dad needed to 'relocate'.

By the time I arrived, Dad had already made himself some allies in the Ballateri family, the main mafia crew in Allentown. They had owed some serious money to a London firm who were very close to Dad. Joe introduced Dad to Pete Ballateri, the head of the family, and together they worked the problem out. Dad has always had a knack for persuading debtors to cough up and he soon proved a few thousand miles of ocean was no obstacle to getting a result for his friends. A few meetings and phone calls later, the job was done and Dad had made some new allies. He always manages to grease the wheels.

Joe and Dave Rosen were keen for Dad to help run

and expand the business and my arrival meant another man was on the firm to keep it growing. Thanks to our pool-table days, Dad and I were old hands at putting machines in bars and collecting the takings, and we took to the slight variation on a theme like ducks to water. We drove around all the towns within the New York–Atlantic City–Philly triangle, and were soon taking a good cut of money for our efforts. Our English charm seemed to work wonders on the various bar and hotel owners we spoke to. They loved our 'funny accents', and were only too happy to take machines and benefit from the protection offered by our formidable associates.

Driving around gave me a taste of how big America is. You really have no idea until you live there – we were only covering a tiny pocket of a vast country, but the distances involved were still huge. On working days we'd cover hundreds of miles – a far cry from our old 'rounds' back in London. People would ask us to supply a couple of pinball machines for their bar. 'Where are you?' we'd ask. 'Just up the road,' they'd say, but 'up the road' would be a two-hour drive away. In the first few weeks, Dad and I had a wonderful time giving our eyes a treat and thinking about how we might carve ourselves a bigger slice of the pie in the games-machine business. We were always looking for angles, and sooner or later we hoped to find something to provide much more substantial paydays.

I look back on that period with fond memories. America was new and exciting, and I was delighted to have Dad to myself for such long stretches of time. I think he felt the same way too. Back home we'd always been surrounded by so many people – family, friends, the chaps – and I'd loved that, but now it really was just the two of us. It was a wonderful chance for us to really get to know each other as men.

At first we lived at close quarters in Dad's condo. Dad had the bedroom, I had a sofa bed. We spent a lot of time just chilling out and doing what men do best – eating, watching movies, talking and laughing. We were like *The Odd Couple* – minus the tension of course – with me doing a Felix, the Jack Lemmon character, constantly cleaning and preparing meals in the kitchen. I've always loved cooking, and for the first couple of months I was the chef in our little condo-cum-diner. With no women around to tell us what to eat, we always went for our favourites. Night after night we'd wolf down huge bowls of spaghetti Bolognese. If there was left-over sauce I'd add chillies and beans – hey presto, I had a chilli con carne for the next day's lunch. Broiled steaks and jacket potatoes was another regular. Whatever we ate was always washed down with a couple of bottles of red, and it was pretty damn wonderful. The trouble was we weren't getting any exercise, and all the good living soon began to take its toll on our waistlines. Before we knew it, we were massive. I ballooned to nearly 15 stone. And Dad – well, I won't mention his weight gain!

'Look at the size of us,' we'd say. I'll never forget how I used to make Dad laugh whenever I stood behind a door, stick my huge belly out and whistle the tune from *Alfred Hitchcock Presents*. Another thing that never failed to tickle him was my impression of the Phantom Raspberry Blower of Old London Town from *The Two Ronnies*. It was a Spike Milligan idea: a Jack the Ripper-style madman used to roam the Victorian streets and stun his victims by blowing raspberries. In my version the Allentown Raspberry Blower would strike whenever Dad was going into one about something or other. Dad had an endearing habit of getting worked up while watching the American news. 'That's a fucking liberty,' he'd say, red-faced about something that had no bearing on us – increasing taxes, for instance – and I'd respond with a great big raspberry. It got him every time. Still does. Humour really bonded us while we were finding our feet in those early weeks.

We'd go out drinking together and, alongside all the laughter, we had some proper heart-to-hearts. Serious conversations about the past, present and future. For the first time I asked Dad about many of the things I'd always wanted to know about his life, and he spoke to me openly and honestly, man to man. When younger, it's true to say I had sometimes wondered how and why Dad did the things he'd done. It was only natural and

Dad understood. From those frank conversations I coloured in all the blank spaces and joined up all the dots about the man who had always been my hero.

Dad had done things many would consider terrible, and I've already explained that those acts were part and parcel of the world he lived in. But it was only now that he told me how he really felt about the consequences of his actions. His years away in prison had been painful for him, as they had for me, and his emotional openness about the past was a revelation. Dad's only regrets were centred on what mattered to him most: the effect it had on his family. I discovered nuances of light and shade in him that I'd never noticed before. Beneath that unflappable, tough exterior lies a deeply thoughtful, caring man.

When I was young, I'd often felt anger that my father wasn't with me. His absence caused me so much heartache. I missed him so deeply and, most of all, I blamed those who'd taken him away. That boy took a lot on his shoulders and the authorities became my scapegoat. Yet there's no denying I knew Dad was being held for a reason: he'd done 'bad' things. Dad would be the first to agree that he wouldn't have gone to jail were it not for his actions, and as a boy I had moments of anger towards him for not being around. I was angry that what he'd done had led to the family being torn apart. I couldn't help it.

At the same time, I knew how much he loved us all

and I felt guilty for blaming anything on my father. Even when Dad returned to us, that guilt never left me. It wasn't until now, years later, that I was finally able to admit my true feelings. I explained everything and Dad understood perfectly. He'd felt his share of guilt about hurting us kids too, and those intimate conversations put a lot of ghosts to bed for both of us.

Those early days in Allentown gave each of us a chance to learn what the other was really about. Dad had always been prepared to pay the price for his actions, and if it came to it he was prepared to do the same again. I came to understand him as a man who needed to fulfil his own destiny – if Dad didn't live life his way, he wouldn't have been the fantastic father he was. Fencing himself in, becoming tamed and trying to live a 'normal' life would have wiped out his self-esteem. And a father without self-esteem is no father at all. Dad told me he would never promise to give us a worry-free life, as it was a promise he knew he could not keep. I understood this perfectly, especially because I was beginning to realise I didn't want a worry-free life.

A rich life is filled with uncertainty, with peaks and troughs, with good times and bad. Growing up a Foreman, and looking at the lives of others, the highs seemed higher and the lows seemed lower. But, as a result, I'd learned to take things as they came, to roll with the punches and enjoy the buzz of living life on the edge. It also struck me that acting was a career where nothing is for certain. Rather like Dad's world, you never know what's around the corner. One minute you could have your name in lights, the next be unemployed, sitting on the sofa watching daytime television. That unpredictability is half the excitement. Speaking with Dad, I came to understand how a fear of the unknown makes you feel more alive.

I believe that Dad's devotion to me during that period was his way of saying sorry for all the time we'd been apart. We became true mates, the best of friends. It was one of the most wonderful things that ever happened to me. We made up for those painful lost years, and then some. I don't know many men who've been lucky enough to share such closeness with their fathers. I will always feel blessed for the opportunity I had to understand – and be understood by – my dearest dad.

After a few months of helping out old man Rosen, a business opportunity arose. A premises became available on Hamilton Boulevard, the main drag in downtown Allentown. Dad, Joe and I realised we'd found the angle we were looking for. It was a huge old building with a Wild West-style frontage. The ground floor had recently been an office-furniture showroom, and at the back there was a warehouse. We thought the whole lot would be perfect as a games room. Thanks to Rosen, we obtained a licence and set up shop. The doors opened and we were soon doing a very, very brisk trade, pulling in hundreds of dollars a day.

We'd filled the room with the most state-of-the-art slot and games machines. Down one side we had about 15 pinball machines and all the brand-new video games – Asteroids, Space Invaders and Pac-Man – in the prime positions. Before I'd left for Tenerife all those months back, people were marvelling at electronic table tennis, but these games were out of this world. And they took a fortune at a quarter (25 cents) a game. Whenever anyone played, a crowd would gather around to watch. At the rear we had six full-size American pool tables and an air-hockey machine.

Allentown had plenty of kids with nothing to do, so we always had a crowd in. And what a bunch of characters they were. Our clientele weren't the most sophisticated bunch. It was soon clear that we'd mainly be dealing with a lot of feisty souls from the wrong side of the tracks. We had the lot, from white trailer trash to unemployed black kids and rowdy Puerto Ricans. Our customers were a handful from the off. A right lairy lot. They'd come in with their quarters and spend their days pumping them into our machines – just what we wanted, of course. Trouble was, different factions and gangs would constantly squabble and fight. But worse still was the liberties that were taken with our machines. Bad losers would kick and shake our very expensive equipment and that showed a total lack of respect.

Dad and I knew how to run a business, and we wouldn't be taken for a ride. The Foreman name was well known in London and as a result Dad's premises had always been safe, trouble-free places. But we had no such notoriety in Allentown. Not yet, anyway. These people thought they could take the piss. How wrong they were. We never took any shit back home, and we weren't about to take it here. The Foreman reputation had to be established.

Being Londoners, we were quick off the mark when it came to dealing with trouble. If a punter kicked a machine, they were told to fuck off out of it in no uncertain terms. The threat of getting barred sufficed much of the time, as they never had anywhere else to go. At first, however, people didn't know what 'getting barred' meant. A funny example of America and England being divided by a common language.

Many of the kids fancied themselves and didn't take us seriously to start with. I'd give someone a bollocking, only to get a load of jive talk – it was the seventies, remember – spat back at me. Perhaps people thought we were soft touches because we were English and had 'funny voices', perhaps it was something else that drove them. Either way, those who fronted up to Dad and me soon learned they were mouthing off to the wrong people.

When dealing with certain situations, there's sometimes nothing for it but to show people what you're made of. In the early days we had to throw many a right-hander at those mouthy bastards. That was a language they did understand. I didn't like doing it, but it was the only way to maintain order. At first I was chinning one of them every other day. But, lo and behold, we soon began to get the respect we deserved.

That said, the hassle never stopped. Predictably, those we had barred would try to come back in and get aggressive when told they were on probation. Time and again some black dude would square up to me and, once again, I'd lay him out. I'd never been much of a fighter up until then, and I never chinned anyone who didn't ask for it, but putting it about became the only way to survive.

On the positive side, being on my feet and dealing with all that grief meant I had to lose that belly of mine – we joined the YMCA gym and Dad trained me up with a lot of bag and ring work. Before long, I was as fit as a butcher's dog and back to my fighting weight. I had a couple of close calls now and again, but normally Dad and I were on each other's shoulder, so we were able to match whatever was thrown at us. But there was one occasion when I really thought I'd met my match.

It was a Saturday morning. I'd been out the night before and was very hung-over. A bloke came in with his son – a harmless little white kid with glasses – left him with a bunch of quarters and headed off shopping. While his Dad was gone, some of the black kids started to give the boy a hard time, nicked his money and the little boy ran out crying.

The first thing I knew about it was when his father came back. He was a giant. He looked like an American footballer – a real man-mountain – and suddenly I found myself being screamed at by this very angry, scary-looking bastard.

'You stood by and watched my little boy getting robbed,' he yelled. 'You let this happen and I want my money back.'

He was effing and blinding something chronic and unfortunately there was no reasoning with him. I could tell he wanted to have it, but frankly I didn't fancy my chances with a six-foot-four brick shithouse. He was calling me everything under the sun and I was getting a little nervous. The last thing I wanted to do was steam into this guy – he looked like he'd eat me for breakfast. But I couldn't back down in front of everyone either. So I kept trying to reason with him.

'There's no need to call me names,' I said. Stern but polite.

He paused for a second. Then he took a step back. 'You're right,' he said, suddenly all humble. 'I'm sorry for being so rude.'

This was a little confusing. I wasn't quite sure what I'd done, but it seemed to be working. With every second he became more apologetic, his massive frame shrinking away from me. My confidence began to rise.

'Another thing. You shouldn't have left your son in here in the first place,' I said, taking a step forward. 'And I think it's time for you to leave.'

He nodded nervously, and told me everything I said was true. I was winning this contretemps and becoming ever braver. The bloke was backing off in a hurry, and soon we were at the door.

'So,' I added, feeling pretty pleased with myself, 'fuck off out of here and don't ever come back.'

Strong words, for sure, but I thought his rudeness deserved them. Thankfully, he turned and beat a hasty retreat down the street. Result, I thought. I'd never been so relieved to see the back of someone. At the same time I was shocked I'd got away with it so easily. I guess it made me feel pretty smug.

I turned to walk back inside, and it was only then that I realised the truth behind my triumph. Behind me stood another very large man, a hard-as-nails Hell's Angel with the meanest look on his face and a huge knuckleduster wrapped around his clenched fist. It was Tyce, the head of the local chapter and a very good man. Tyce and I were good friends. The penny dropped right away. The father wasn't scared of me one bit until my leather-clad, bearded bruiser of a mate showed his face. I burst out laughing. What a good man Tyce was. Always a man of few words, he'd sat on my shoulder with quiet composure, knowing it was all he needed to do. I've always treasured that moment. He also backed my dad up on one occasion when it looked like he was outnumbered. We were both very fond of Tyce.

Tyce and I also became hotshots on the pool table. We did a roaring trade in hustling, playing 'three-handed carve-up' for money. He'd set me up, I'd set him up, and together we'd wipe the floor with anyone who took us on. We used to cut up 50 dollars each on a good day – a very nice little drink back then.

As was the way of our world, we always took care of our own problems. We never called the police for help, and for that the local *gendarmerie* was grateful. Our relationship with the cops was good as gold. It was a proud moment for Dad and I when one day some officers came in and congratulated us for running such a tight ship in such a troublesome area. When we'd opened up they'd expected to be called out every five minutes. Little did they know they were the last people we wanted to have anything to do with.

By way of thanks, Dad and I used to contribute to their social and charitable functions, which kept them sweet. Cops everywhere never fail to appreciate a case of Scotch. It was always amusing when one of the black dudes would come in, cause trouble, get a belting, then call in the law to try and get *us* nicked. On many occasions a cop would show up, look at my exasperated face and give me a sly wink – they knew the type of people we were dealing with and the matter would always end there. We were lucky in that respect. According to the US constitution, defending your property by any means is a God-given right.

Ironically, the only difficulty we ever had with the police was nothing to do with our business. On reflection, it makes me laugh, but at the time it could have been a very dangerous situation. One night Dad and I were driving home from a bar in Easton, a nearby town, where we had a couple of pontoon gambling machines. The bar was owned by Larry Holmes, the former World Heavyweight Boxing Champion. On the way home I suddenly realised that nature was calling. It would be a long drive home and there was no way I could wait. Dad pulled over at a gas station and, realising it was closed, I nipped round the side of the building to relieve myself. I'd just unzipped when I suddenly heard the screech of tyres on tarmac. The next thing I knew I was fully illuminated by a spotlight. It was the police. I looked round to see a copper leaning over the door of his squad car with a .38 pistol pointed straight at me. It was just like something out of *Starsky & Hutch*. This wasn't the first time I'd had a gun pointed at me by the law – I had a flashback to that morning back in Dulwich. Here we go again, I thought.

'Put your hands up,' yelled the officer.

I was in a rather compromising position – I was reluctant to raise my hands as, with a gun trained on me, I was finding it a little hard to refrain from peeing.

Shouting over my shoulder, I did my best to explain my predicament to the increasingly nervous copper. Eventually, by the time he had screamed at me for the third time, I was finally able to stick up my hands. I zipped myself up and walked towards him, hands in the air.

'I'm terribly sorry, officer,' I said in my poshest English accent. 'I'm a tourist from London, England. I was suddenly caught short...'

I sensed the officer calming down a little. 'Walk toward me and get out your ID,' he barked suspiciously.

'No problem,' I replied calmly. But out of the corner of my eye, I noticed my dad getting out of the car and walking up behind the cop. His hand was thrust into the inside of his jacket – he was obviously reaching for his ID – and I could see his mouth moving but there was no sound coming out. Suddenly I remembered Dad had lost his voice. Shit, I thought, the copper's going to think he's being crept up on and that Dad's reaching for a gun. Carefully I explained that my dad was approaching from the rear, couldn't speak and was searching for his ID. I was desperate for the copper not to panic.

Luckily he didn't. But he did look a bit confused. He asked us to clarify who we were. We did. Finally he lowered his gun. It turned out there'd been a recent spate of robberies at various gas stations in the area – the police had spotted Dad's car and assumed the worst.

Fortunately we managed to convince him we were innocent and didn't do anything rash. It was all over. Realising all was well, the policeman got chatty.

'I've got a friend in Liverpool who runs a fish and chip shop,' he said. 'Do you guys know it?'

Now Liverpool's a big place with hundreds of chippies, a fact our uniformed friend didn't seem to appreciate.

'Yeah, sure we do,' said Dad, giving me a wink. 'Lovely place on the corner, right?'

'That's right. So it is,' said the cop.

Anything to get rid of them, eh?

Life in the games room was pretty repetitive. There were always hassles to sort out and Dad and I were at the front line. You couldn't let your guard down for a second. Staying sharp was sometimes tough, not to mention boring. Both of us felt that way. Still, it was better than being banged up back in Britain.

There were other consolations too, one of them being money. We were making a fortune. Aside from the games room – which brought in very tidy profits – Dad's ever-expanding connections in Allentown and beyond gave him some very nice touches. Several enterprises were doing very nicely indeed. As a result he soon had enough funds to start building us a new family home in preparation for Mum and Danni's move from England. Very conscious of what a huge upheaval America was for us all, he wanted to give us the best life possible. He heard about a new 'private' development that was being planned in a wonderful location on the outskirts of Allentown. He laid down a deposit for a house to be built in the Georgian style. There would be three bedrooms, all with en suite, a large den with a stunning open stone fireplace, lounge and separate dining room, double garage, a swimming pool and a beautiful garden filled with cherry and peach trees. Work was soon under way.

Another positive for me was the girls. My English-gent manners worked wonders on American ladies, and I was an instant hit with the women. I was never short of a date and had a ball going out to all the best bars and clubs. I knew all the owners, so never had any trouble with the under-21 rule – not that they tended to be much younger than that, I hasten to add! – and always made a point of holding doors open and pulling chairs out. That's the way us English do things, but many of the girls I met simply weren't used to being treated so nicely. The results were astonishing and I had some wonderful evenings with some very liberal young ladies.

Dad and I had made a good name for ourselves in Allentown and were welcomed by black and white folk alike. Segregation was long gone, but the different ethnic groups still tended to stick to their own. Most of the bars and clubs were either 'black' or 'white', but we felt very privileged to be welcomed in either. I've many fond memories of nights out as the only white face in a black crowd, but those evenings were only possible because of the goodwill we'd earned through a combination of business and friendship – two things that had always mixed in our world back home.

It's said that 'Home is where the heart is' and it was painful for Mum and Dad to finally sell our wonderful house in Dulwich. After Mum completed the sale, she and Danni made their way to Allentown. We hadn't seen them in five months and our reunion was as wonderful as can be imagined. Dad had moved us to a new, larger condo and Mum lost no time in turning it into a lovely home for us to stay in until the new house was completed.

Allentown was a shock for Mum and Danni, as it had been for me. Being away from friends and family was undeniably hard on the girls, but as always they made the best out of the situation. We were all in this together. We knew it wasn't for ever, so there was nothing else for it but to be thankful for family life, knuckle down and get on with it. Danni found a job with the local theatre company and was soon having a whale of a time in several productions. I think she enjoyed the experience really. She made new friends. Scott, a good-looking young gay guy, was her real 'buddy'. He was a lovely kid and idolised Danni. We helped her get a part-time job in a clothes shop in the local shopping mall, and Dad gave her the use of our truck – a huge Dodge pick-up that she absolutely adored. It really was something to watch the way she handled that beast, and we soon gave her the nickname 'Trucker Dan'. It was good to see her happy – like me, my Danni had been through a hell of a lot over the years.

And why didn't I get involved in a bit of acting? I was too busy bringing home the bacon with Dad. Providing for the family always came first.

Eventually, our beautiful house was ready to move into. The whole family adored it. For the first time since leaving our beloved house in Dulwich, we were in a place we could *really* call home. I cherished the moments spent together in our new house. For me home life was as fine as it could be. But as the year wore on my life outside that home slowly began to unravel.

Day in, day out, Dad and I minded the games room. At first I'd been happy with it all – setting up and establishing control had been a real challenge, a battle I'd enjoyed fighting. But nothing ever changed after that – it was the same old same old. The same faces, the same old squabbles, the same threats and jibes and the same old right-handers to keep trouble at bay. I was winging it every day of the week and over time the repetition started to wear me down. When it came to our customers, my fuse got shorter and shorter. I was well used to their petty displays of bravado – at first I'd found their small-town mentality a mere surface nuisance – but now the ignorant, unworldly ways of our punters was really getting under my skin. I wanted to be an artist on stage. Hanging around with these lowlifes was a constant reminder of how starved I was creatively.

Often, as I stood around listening to the endless quarters dropping into our machines, I thought of my old life in London. How I missed the places I'd seen and the fascinating, diverse world of entertainment I was part of. My friends had been actors, directors, artists – people with ideas and dreams. What a contrast they were to the crowd in this place. It seemed our punters dreamed of little more than a free game of Space Invaders.

I became directionless and dejected. All the hopes and ambitions I held felt like nothing more than a pipedream. I would never reach my full potential stuck in this place, and that realisation made me feel very depressed. But I bottled up my emotions for the sake of the family. We all had our worries. I sensed the claustrophobia of the games room was getting to Dad too, and Mum and Danni had become increasingly homesick. We all had to do our bit and stay strong for each other. I kept telling myself it wasn't for ever and tried to remain positive. After all, we had a house, friends and money and, most importantly, our freedom – all reasons to be cheerful. Still, I couldn't put the brakes on my unhappiness. Slowly but surely the cracks began to show.

My frustration inevitably turned to anger. I'm sorry to say that I started taking it out on others. Simple as they were, the guys at the games room couldn't help it. They came from tough, deprived backgrounds and hanging out and ducking and diving was as good as it was going to get for them. Those guys were our bread and butter too. Without their quarters our business didn't exist. But knowing that didn't stop me from starting to hate those around me – I needed another scapegoat and unfortunately I found it in our customers.

At first I'd only got physical if somebody was taking a liberty, but all of a sudden – much to my horror – I found myself *wanting* to have a row over the littlest things. Comments that normally would have been water off a duck's back were rankling with me big time. I was picking fights for no good reason. I got more and more feisty and the change in my demeanour made me very uncomfortable. Worst of all, I couldn't do anything about it.

Even Dad was shocked by my unpredictable outbursts. I remember walking into the office one day to relieve him from a morning shift. Sitting with Dad was a guy I'd thrown out the previous day. Without saying a word I walked up and punched him in the eye. One minute Dad had been talking to him and now the bloke was clutching his face in agony. Dad was shocked.

'What was that about?' he said.

'I fucking barred him yesterday,' I yelled, pumped up and angry. 'I kicked him up the arse and slung him out.'

Always fair, Dad thought I'd gone over the top and told me so. I calmed down, and felt ashamed for talking back to my own father. I apologised and that was the end of it. Looking back, I should have taken my outburst as a warning that there was worse to come. But I didn't. I certainly could not have predicted what I would end up doing a couple of months later. But I think that moment in the office was a sign to Dad that something was wrong. It certainly wasn't lost on him. This wasn't the Jamie he knew, and it worried him.

One day we heard a whisper: a gang were planning to rob us. The stick-up crew would be armed. This was bad fucking news and very troubling. Up until then we'd been happy to steer clear of guns – they'd caused us enough trouble in the past and we had no need for them in our line of work. But, knowing our fists would be useless against firearms, we decided to acquire a couple of shooters from the local chaps. We bought an automatic and a revolver. There was a lot of money at stake and we had to be tooled up in case of the worst.

We didn't have a gun licence, so couldn't carry loaded weapons, but there was a way around that. In America you could carry a gun if you keep the bullets in one pocket and the gun in another. Licence or no licence, you couldn't get nicked for it. We kept the .32 automatic locked in a drawer at work, but sometimes I'd walk around with it, the clip in one pocket and the piece in the other. I felt safer that way.

Time passed and thankfully the robbers never showed. But locking up one night we heard someone trying a back door. Dad drew the automatic, cocked it and shouted through the door that he was going to fire. We gave it a second and charged out. Whoever it was must have legged it. A false alarm, perhaps, or maybe the crew realised we weren't to be fucked with. Who knows? Following that, I kept the tool close at hand as I went about my angry days in the games room.

By now I'd been doing the same job for nearly a year and it was really sapping my resolve. I was constantly on edge and my state of mind only worsened. The lower I got, the more I tried to fight it and keep myself on an even keel. But I was fighting a personal battle – and losing. The pressure in my head mounted; I was a bomb waiting to go off. Then, one terrible day, I exploded.

For once the games room wasn't busy. There was no need for me to stand around, so I took a rest in the back office. I was in a reflective mood, dreaming of England. How I wished I were back home. My mates were there, my career was there – or had been – and life in Allentown had nothing left to offer me. I was melancholy as hell.

Just then a man came bursting into my office. It was Tyrone, one of the local faces, a real character who did a good line in nicked gear. He was always out thieving and I used to help him shift whatever he pinched. He was six foot two and a right funny bastard, so I'd always had a bit of affection for him. We got on well. Tyrone stood out from the others and always amused me. Today, however, I wasn't in the mood.

Full of himself as ever, Tyrone waltzed in on a high: he'd nicked a load of designer shirts. 'Look at this lot,' he babbled excitedly, assuming I'd be interested. I wasn't. I didn't give a fuck about Tyrone and his shirts. 'We'd better shift these,' he said, holding out one of them. 'Help me take the pins out.'

And then he threw it at me.

I can barely remember what happened next. All I know is that I lost it. Within seconds of that shirt hitting my chest, I was out of my chair, across the room and pointing my cocked .32 automatic against Tyrone's head. A red mist had descended over me and I completely flipped out. I growled every swear word under the sun into his wide-eyed, terrified face: I was going to maim him, I was going to put one in his nut, I was going to bury him; he was a nigger, he was a punk, he was a cunt. Terrible, terrible words, I know, but I was in a terrible way.

Tyrone shook as I ranted, and tried in vain to calm me down. His words were no use – I'd truly lost it. For the first time in my life I wanted to kill and I came terrifyingly close. I remember thinking how easy it would be to pull the trigger and be done with it, with him, with everything. Worse, I remember feeling capable of it. I had it in me.

Thank God I came far enough down to earth to realise

what I was doing. Not that I calmed down right away. Far from it. Still seething, I fired off another volley of insults and slung Tyrone out of the building. When he was gone, I looked down at my hands. I wasn't even shaking.

I hadn't given a thought to the position I could have put us all in. What if he called the cops? But he's a thief, I thought. He won't go to the police. I'd pulled a gun on an Allentown face for no good reason and possibly opened a can of worms. I knew there might be a comeback, but right then I didn't give a fuck. Let him do what he had to do, I thought, I'll fucking have him...

Eventually, the adrenalin died down. Calmer now, I walked back to the office, my head down. What had I done? I'd completely lost control. Simple as that. I'd threatened to end a man's life over a shirt, for fuck's sake – *a shirt*. I'd flipped. I was shocked at myself. Disgusted, confused and shaken. I knew what had happened, but didn't understand why. I'd work that bit out later. Right now there was a situation to deal with.

I picked up the phone and called Dad to explain what had gone down. 'You'd better get down here,' I said. 'It's serious.'

Dad came over like a shot, revolver tucked into his waistband. In situations like that you never know how soon the comeback will happen.

I felt numb. I was so ashamed of myself. It was bad enough that I'd lost the plot, but I felt sick to think I'd created a reputation and put my dad in danger. Rather than an asset to the business, I suddenly felt I was a risk to our safety and well-being. It made me feel like shit. I apologised profusely to Dad, but he was wonderful about it. We sat together and talked it over. I shook my head in disbelief every time I thought about what I'd done. Dad stayed with me for an hour or so.

'These things happen,' he said calmly. 'It's not the end of the world. Still, I think you should go home. I don't think Tyrone will come back now – he's probably shitting himself. Take the afternoon off. '

I didn't want to leave Dad on his own, but he reassured me he would be all right and insisted I rest. So I went.

I'd really scared myself. I was shaken to the core by what I'd nearly done. Never had I felt remotely capable of doing such a thing. But my behaviour made me realise I'd got myself wrong. I was capable of anything. During those moments with Tyrone I'd glimpsed that dark place in my soul – a place that I feel any man can go if pushed – and, while I learned something about myself, it terrified me. The hatred I felt towards my situation had led me to hate others. My actions in that office made me start to feel very uncomfortable about myself. I realised what I had become. I wasn't the man I thought I was, nor the man I wanted to be.

Back at the house, Mum comforted me. I have always been able to unload on Mum. I still do today. She opened some wine and we talked about the way I'd been feeling over the last 18 months – the stress I'd been under – and I told her how I'd been bottling it all up. I needed to understand why I'd lost control that badly, and Mum's wisdom and love helped me accept that I wasn't a bad person. My situation had turned me into a caged animal and eventually something had snapped. It wasn't Tyrone I'd been trying to destroy, it was what he represented. Tyrone was just one of my jailers in a life that had imprisoned me.

My situation had come to a head. The incident was proof I needed a change. Having discussed it with Mum, Dad was the first to recognise it. It upset him to realise I'd got to a place in my head where I might end up doing similar things to those he'd done in the past. It broke his heart to think I might do something rash and have to pay the price in prison. He'd always loved my help, but he'd never wanted my life to go the way of his. Just as I'd always wanted to be there for him, he wanted to be there for me now that I needed it.

Our journey had been long. Together we had started from scratch and made a success of America, but it couldn't go on for ever. I could no longer see the wood for the trees and, with nothing but my best interests in mind, Dad decided enough was enough.

'I know what you've been through,' he told me one night. 'I've found it tough myself. But this is my life. You have your career and *your* life to think about. I think you should start thinking about going back to England.'

Dad had recently got word from the chaps that it would be safe for me to slip back – the poor Customs man's murder case was over and the hunt for Dad was dying down. The authorities had realised that I'd had nothing to do with planning to bring the drugs in.

Much as I missed my old life, the idea of leaving Dad again filled me with fear. We'd relied on each other so much in America – for months we'd stood shoulder to shoulder on the lookout for danger – and I was scared of leaving him vulnerable. Dad and I have an inextricable bond and those months together had brought us closer than ever. Looking at him then, sensing the compassion and kinship in his eyes, I loved him more than ever.

But I also felt guilty. Allentown was a prison for Dad too. The idea of abandoning my father brought back all the sickening, horrible feelings from Leicester jail all those years ago. We'd come so far since those dark days – we were together, free and strong – but sometimes those buried emotions came back. I'd lost my father and found him again and I never wanted to let him go. I thought that leaving him would be disloyal in some way. I told Dad how I felt.

He understood. He felt the same way as me – he never wanted to let me go again either. Our time in America had been so precious. We learned more about each other than a father and son could ever hope to. We'd witnessed each other strong and weak; revealed our love through words and actions. Going on the run had been a blessing in disguise. I looked at Dad and smiled. I hadn't failed, I wasn't weak. But the time to move on had come.

'You've done more than your bit, Jamie,' said Dad. 'I'm proud of you. We all are. I'll be fine here, you'll see. But it's time for you to think about yourself. It's time for you to go home, son.'

POSTSCRIPT

On the plane I ordered a Bloody Mary. I paid and as I took my change from the stewardess – a dollar bill – I noticed some writing on it: 'DUKE'. I stared in disbelief. It was Dukey's signature. Impossible, I thought. But there was no mistaking Pasha's hand – I had read his suicide letter. He always wrote in capitals. I was stunned and overwhelmed – all the memories came flooding back. I thought of Duke, of Dad, of 'Scatty Eddie' and his life sentence, and reeled at the enormity of the adventure we'd been through. Poor old Dukey, I thought, a tear coming to my eye. I'd been through so much – we'd all been through so much. Through all the trials and tribulations of our lives, our family had made it this far. To me Dukey's dollar was a sign, his way of telling me that all would be well.

And it was. Getting back to London was like being shot with a wonderful, calming drug. Seeing my mates and reconnecting with the chaps was an injection of pure comfort. But getting back into acting was the icing on the cake. My agent, Bill Horne, had waited patiently and even opened a bank account in my name for my royalty payments, bless him. Before long I was back nicking parts as if I'd never been away. Bliss. I'd been so starved for so long and being back on the fringe circuit made me feel alive again. Moments before going on stage I'd sometimes think back to those days in the games room – of all those quarters dropping, all those battles – and smile as I waited to step out into the spotlight. What an incredible journey I'd been on. Now I had some distance from it, Allentown would always have a place in my heart.

I paid a few more visits to America until Dad finally made it home in 1981. In the end he missed England as badly as I did. Besides, some rival firms he had close links to were rowing, and it was time for Fred to step in and sort things out. A face as powerful as Dad's can't hide in London for ever. Eventually, Dad was arrested and charged with importation of cannabis. At Winchester Crown Court a judge gave him a two-year suspended sentence. What a result.

One day while I was with Pandy, I saw a picture of a beautiful girl in the newspaper. I realised it was Julie immediately. My memory of her was so strong. 'That's Julie Dennis,' I said. 'She slipped the net.'

Anyway, a week later, my sister Danielle, who was working as my PA at the time, told me that she had phoned a friend of hers on her mobile. Asking her where she was, the girl replied, 'I am with a friend of mine, Julie Dennis.' What a coincidence. Now that's what I call fate. When Danni told me, I couldn't believe it. I asked her if Julie was with anyone.

'No, I don't think she is.'

'Then go to work, Danni,' I told her.

Danielle got me her number and within a few days I was speaking to Julie on the phone. It was as if we had only just spoken the week before. I invited her for dinner at my favourite restaurant, J. Sheekey in St Martin's Court. I was so pleased when she said she'd love to.

That night, I felt like a nervous schoolboy as I sat chatting at the bar with my very good old friend Tower, who is a manager there. I actually had butterflies as I downed another Bombay Sapphire and tonic, desperately trying to keep calm. Then she arrived. She looked stunning. It was like the Southwark Park Tavern all over again. She was even more beautiful than I remembered.

'I bet that's her?' Tower asked, as taken as I was.

'Ooh yes.'

'You lucky bastard,' he said, rather unprofessionally.

'Luck's got nothing to do with it,' I replied, laughing.

I ordered her a glass of champagne. Tower showed us to my table and, over a dinner we hardly touched, we just talked and talked. It was wonderful. That night I fell in love with her all over again. Julie and I have been together ever since – over nine years now. We belong together and our wonderful friendship and love have made me the happiest man in the world. She will always be the love of my life, for the rest of my life.

Life was never dull during my first 24 years as a Foreman. What an understatement. It was a non-stop rollercoaster ride through heaven and hell and somewhere in between. Looking back, I wouldn't change a thing. The same applies to everything that would happen in the years following our return to London. Our family would rise and fall, then rise again. History would repeat itself in ways that were too close for comfort. I'd even have to go on my toes again, but I would always bounce back. But that, as they say, is another story ...